By the Best-Selling Authors of

THE 5-DAY TURNAROUND & WHAT DOES YOUR FORTUNE COOKIE SAY?

Part of The Turnaround Leadership Series

THE CULTURE TURNAROUND

9 proven ways to create an undeniable culture

JEFF HILIMIRE
ADAM ALBRECHT

"This book lays out the plan for building a winning culture!"
— Shannon Watkins, Global CMO, Jordan Brand at Nike

First printing 2022

Book cover designed by Michael Stanley

Book interior designed by Andrew Vogel

ISBN 978-1-7338689-9-0

Published by Ripples Media

www.ripples.media

"The purpose of life is to contribute in some way to making things better."

—Robert F. Kennedy

DEDICATION

Jeff

To all the amazing teammates I've shared over the years: at Spunlogic, Engauge, Dragon Army, Ripples Media, 48in48, The A Pledge, Ripples of Hope, and Central Outreach & Advocacy Center.

And of course, to my family: Emily, Zac, Drew, Kaitlyn, Hannah, and Kai. You're my everything.

Adam

To my teammates from Engauge, where we created a great culture together. And to my teammates at The Weaponry, for adding to our culture every day.

CONTENTS

FOREWORD

Culture Starts with an Engaged and Invested Team

I'm not a huge fan of rules. Creative people as a species are naturally averse to them. But if you want to develop a business with a strong culture you need some rules to guide you.

Jeff and I met each other and became friends in 2008 when my agency, TenUnited, joined Spunlogic, Jeff's agency. When our agencies merged, they became part of the same super agency called Engauge. This is fun in theory. But it also creates real challenges. There are always major differences in company cultures. There are different processes, traditions, and norms. Plus, people become concerned about their own positions, status, autonomy, and future opportunities.

This all means that when two organizations combine through a merger, acquisition, or magic trick, the culture is vulnerable. It's difficult enough to establish a strong culture at one singular company. Now imagine trying to maintain a positive culture when two companies merge together! It's a real challenge, even if both previous cultures were strong and positive.

(Also, while this foreword centers on Jeff's and my experiences in establishing a strong culture in the midst of a merger of two companies, the lessons and takeaways are applicable to any organization at any stage. These tools and resources to culture building are relevant regardless of how big or small your company is.)

Going back to the formation of Engauge, it's a little bit like the Reese's Peanut Butter Cup Effect. On their own, peanut butter and chocolate are completely unbound. There are no limitations to what they can do or the form they take. But when they are combined into a peanut butter cup, they are both constrained in order to make the new form work. Peanut butter must play the inside role. Chocolate has to form the outside, ridged shell. Otherwise, the new form doesn't work. The key takeaway—what you should chew on from this confectionary analogy—is that even in a great new culture, there are things that remain from the old culture and things that have to change.

When organizations combine, or when there are personnel or leadership changes, there is an interesting tug of war that takes place. People will pull, advocate, lobby, or fight for control over how the organization will operate moving forward. Those people are fighting to keep things as similar as possible in the new organization to the way they were in the organization they came from. Because it feels familiar. And familiar feels like a win.

Then there are the pure culture champions. These are the people who simply want to create a positive, collaborative, fun, productive environment for all. They are not trying to be territorial. Nor are they precious about the past. They just want to create a great place to work.

There is something special about the culture champions. They are drawn to each other like magnets. And in the first meetings and get-to-know-yous we had following the "You are the chocolate to my peanut butter" moment of our merger, Jeff and I found each other.

I noticed Jeff in those very first introductions and I knew he was my culture counterpart. Jeff was a fun, smiley, friendly guy who clearly wanted to make friends with his new teammates.

You could tell that much of the positivity and personality of his organization started with him. So I sought him out as a friend and ally in the new organization.

Together we worked on the softer side of the merger. The human side. The fun side. We found other humans that also supported our interest in fostering a positive, synergistic culture. We also prioritized developing a positive, collaborative atmosphere in all of our offices. Which was an interesting challenge, because the new super agency had offices in Atlanta, Austin, Columbus, Orlando, and Pittsburgh.

I was looking for a way for the entire team to think about our togetherness, our corporate culture, and to set a tone for the fun we planned to have as an organization. I wanted to send a message that we needed to transcend our pasts and our physical distances.

I knew that it was important to stop identifying ourselves as having come from one team or the other. We quickly had to create a sense of belonging, camaraderie, and being one team.

So I developed a silly little word to symbolize our cultural goal: Weness.

Weness was the state of us feeling like we are now a we. Not individuals. Not two teams pitted against each other in competitions. But one cohesive team. It was also a word no one had ever heard before. So it became something we could embrace as part of the new Engauge culture.

Jeff and I spent a lot of time addressing the organization and talking about expectations. We created new norms, traditions, and rituals. We had Weness activities and rewarded Weness behaviors.

When groups from various offices were together and intermixed there were often comments and cheers about Weness, mostly because it sounded funny. But also because it worked. It worked because we prioritized our togetherness, our shared future, and our collaboration.

As you read through this book, while it's not mentioned specifically, look for instances of Weness and why it goes hand in hand with the success of an undeniable culture. Employees are more engaged and committed when there is a purpose to their work—when they're invested in something greater than themselves. This book gives numerous examples of how Weness is fostered by Will and his leadership team, and provides actionable ways in which you can implement the same strategies in your organization.

Fast forward back to Engauge, Jeff and I took our secondary roles as culture champions very seriously. We knew it was imperative to keep our best, most valuable people magnetized to the organization. We knew it had the power to improve the outlook and attitude of some of our more cynical staff members. It would help attract great new talent. And ultimately create a positive, productive work environment that attracted great clients.

And that is exactly what happened.

The strong, positive culture created a flywheel of success. It attracted and retained great people. Those great people attracted great clients, including UPS, Wells Fargo, Coca-Cola, Nationwide Insurance, Universal Studios, and Nike.

In today's market, leaders have to make sure their employees feel valued in order to keep them engaged (get it?). In order to get the best work out of your organizations, you must show each and every team member why their contributions are critical to the solution.

You'll love this book in part because it's a sweet and satisfying read (going back to our Reese's analogy). But also, there are so many tangible examples of how to get the most out of your team members and help them be absolutely invested in their organization's overall success.

If you are looking for ways to positively influence the culture at your company, and how to establish that unique sense of Weness, this book is a great place to start.

Adam Albrecht

CEO, The Weaponry

Author, What Does Your Fortune Cookie Say?

PRELUDE

Here's something you probably didn't expect to hear from me right out of the gate: **I generally dislike business books.**

I know, right? Here you are, holding a business book that I wrote (the fourth one I've written, in fact) and I'm telling you that I dislike them. Bonkers.

Perhaps I should explain :)

This book is the fourth installment of *The Turnaround Leadership Series.* As far as where this book actually falls in the series, well, that will also take a few paragraphs to unpack.

In 2018, I began the process of writing what I thought would be my first and only book. I had a belief that any person could embody the mindset of an entrepreneur and decided the best way to share that with people would be to put it into a book. And so I got to writing....

Only, I was bored with what I was writing. Because, as I shared at the top of this page, I don't actually like the typical business books. I much prefer biographies, where I can learn through the experiences of others.

Which is probably why I've always loved parable-style business books, with Patrick Lencioni being the undisputed champion of that genre. *The Five Dysfunctions of a Team* is a **must** for any leader.

At a certain point I realized that I couldn't very well write a book that I wouldn't enjoy reading, so why not give this parable-style of writing a chance. And thus, Will (the main character) and his friends were born. As I wrote, I obviously put a lot of myself into Will, and I picked and pulled characteristics from my friends to create the rest of the characters you meet in the book.

That first book ended up being called *The 5-Day Turnaround* and, as a first time author, I thought it did very well. And that was that. I wrote a book, some people enjoyed it, now back to life.

Yet those characters kept calling to me. And it turned out that I had more to say. In early 2020 I was in the beginning stages of writing the book you now hold in your hands, but then the coronavirus pandemic changed everything. I found myself grasping for ideas on how to lead my company through this unforeseen crisis. As I spoke to other business leaders, I found that no one seemed to have a playbook for how to lead through a crisis. So I put this book down and wrote my second book, *The Crisis Turnaround.*

I decided to write *The Crisis Turnaround* as a prelude to *The 5-Day Turnaround.* It made more sense to me that Will's company would be a bit smaller and earlier in its development when this crisis hit them. Plus, if George Lucas can release movies in all sorts of weird timelines, then why not me?

And so I picked this book concept back up and began working on it. Then the folks at The Great Game of Business™ reached out to me, after having found some of my blog posts about how much I love their methodology for operating a business, and asked if I would speak at their annual conference. Being a huge fan, I readily agreed. Over the years I had worked hard to marry my leadership principle, called PVTV™ (Purpose, Vision, Tenets, and Values), together with The Great Game of Business™. Through my talk at their conference, I realized that a lot of people were interested in hearing more about that concept.

So, once again I put this book concept down and wrote a different book altogether. The third book in the series became *The Great Team Turnaround.* I used the same cast of characters and this book fell chronologically after the first book. One year after giving my first talk at The Great Game conference, I came back to give a keynote speech, launching book three.

At this point it was late 2021 and I had written three books, and I was bound and determined to write and publish this book in 2022. If you're keeping track at home, the topics thus far were, a) leading like an entrepreneur, b) leading during a crisis, and c) creating a great team. It was time to write about building an undeniable culture.

By this time it also occurred to me that I should collaborate on this book with my good friend (and fellow author) Adam Albrecht. I knew Adam to be as passionate as I am about culture, having worked side by side with him at Engauge for over five years, building what I think became a very special culture.

When we sat down to write this book, it quickly became apparent to us that Will and his team needed to be in Year Three of their business for this story to work, and thus, with the hopes of confusing everyone with the order of these books, *The Culture Turnaround* occurs before all the other books. As the primary author, even I have a tough time keeping it straight at this point, so here's a handy chart to help:

Order of Publication	Order in Story's Timeline
The 5-Day Turnaround	*The Culture Turnaround*
The Crisis Turnaround	*The Crisis Turnaround*
The Great Team Turnaround	*The 5-Day Turnaround*
The Culture Turnaround	*The Great Team Turnaround*

George Lucas, eat your heart out.

It should be pointed out that you don't have to read the books in order. They're written so they each can be read as a standalone book, or you can read them in order, following the growth and troubles of Will's business along the way.

And just to further confuse you, my current plan is to write the fifth (and perhaps final) book in the series in 2023 called, *The Life Turnaround*, focusing on Will's mentor, Charles. Oh, right, and IT WILL TAKE PLACE 30 YEARS BEFORE THE FIRST BOOK! I know, but ...

Thanks for going on this journey with us. We hope you're happy,

THE CULTURE TURNAROUND

CHAPTER 1

Here's the thing about me: I've never really minded pressure.

Maybe I was born with some kind of pressure-resistance, though that seems doubtful. More likely I've been conditioned over time to welcome, and if I'm being honest, in some cases embrace times of stress. Things just seem to come into focus more clearly, with all the fluffy, less important things falling by the wayside.

It wasn't always this way. I remember when I was early in my tennis career, maybe 14 years old, and I made my way through a tennis tournament and ultimately found myself in my first finals. I was just as shocked to be in the finals as my opponent was to see me (he was seeded No. 1 and I was unseeded).

He was even more shocked when I quickly won the first set and took a lead in the second. It was at that point that I realized that I could actually win the tournament, a feat I'd never accomplished before. I started to feel a bit nervous and "tight." In tennis, nervousness leads to your body tightening up. Your feet stop moving and your strokes are less fluid. It wasn't long before my opponent (then much looser because the pressure had shifted to me) began to string together a few games, and ultimately beat me 6-0 in the third set. I was devastated.

Over time, consistently finding myself in pressure situations, I learned that if I leaned into the pressure, I could calm myself and regain my focus. I would take this mentality into my career and then as an entrepreneur, almost looking forward to times of difficulty.

And what is it that people say? Times of stress are when leaders are defined. Perhaps there's a vanity or insecurity inside of me that craves the chance to prove myself. To step up and show that I'm not a fraud; that I deserve to be a leader.

Whatever the reason, I'm good with pressure.

Which is probably why, when I was told by my shareholders that I would most likely be losing control of my business—a business that I had put everything into over the last three years, mind you —my initial thought was, "Game on."

"Will, before we get started with the meeting, we have something we want to discuss with you. Perhaps you should have a seat."

That was James, my Board Chair. Everyone on my board was an investor, and they were all here. I liked them. Though a little less at this particular moment.

In my experience, it's rarely good when a meeting or conversation starts off with someone saying, "We have something we want to discuss with you," and even more rare when they ask you to have a seat. Throughout the course of history when that phrase is used, I'm certain very few ever turned out to be a pleasant surprise.

"William, we have something we want to discuss with you, you might want to sit down for this...we're going to Disney World!"

"Sure, James," I said, sitting back down. "What's up?"

"You know we are your biggest fans, maybe aside from Sarah, of course. And we're all investors in your business, which means we've put our money where our mouths are. We've been so impressed..."

I droned out the rest of the sugarcoating. There was something coming and I wished James would just come out with it. I always appreciated it when someone had the nerve to cut to the chase when a difficult thing needed to be said.

As he finished explaining just how much they all loved me, I sat silently looking back at him. I used to have a problem with jumping in and filling any dead space in a conversation, particularly in an awkward one. Over time I've learned, with a little nudging from my mentor, Charles, to err on the side of silence when possible.

Glancing around the room, I looked at each of my board members. None of them were making eye contact with me. A few of them were looking at James, their eyes urging him to continue.

My attention found its way back to him as he finished. "The thing is, we've been approached by another business that would like to merge with your company," he said.

Huh.

This I was not expecting. We had never discussed as a board even the remote chance of selling the business. And while that was our long-term plan, I would be the one initiating and running the process, with the board acting at best as a sounding board (pardon the pun).

I took a deep breath and asked, "And this other company, who is it?"

"Unfortunately, we aren't at liberty to say. They had us sign a non-disclosure agreement restricting us from sharing their name or the specifics of the deal with anyone, even with you."

Even with me?

No, especially with me.

"That's insane, James! How can I consider a merger if I don't know the company we might merge with?"

He looked at me for a moment, waiting for me to catch up.

"Ah," I said. "I'm not considering this, am I? You are. I'm not really a part of the decision, am I?"

"I wouldn't put it like that," he said. "But we do have the votes to push a sale of the company forward if we want to, as you know."

Yes, thanks, James. I was indeed aware of that fact.

"A sale of the company? Are we talking about a merger or being acquired? Can you at least tell me how big the company that wants to screw me is?" I asked.

"Will, they don't want to screw you, they're just interested in joining forces," Linda said. Linda had been a very successful CFO during her career. She was now retired, on a few boards like mine, and lived on some kind of timeshare cruise ship half of the year. I kind of wished she was on that boat right now.

"The company is local and from what we can gather, about twice the size of yours, Will," said Bruce, jumping into the conversation. Laura looked at him like he had just shared the secret code to Area 51. Glancing around at the rest of the board members, he said, "Come on, he can at least know that we're talking about an acquisition, not really a merger. The company is much bigger, probably a few years ahead of you."

"And they just approached you out of the blue? You weren't shopping around for a deal?!" I asked, barely able to control the rage welling up inside of me.

James said, "No, of course we weren't shopping around. We had no intention of doing this. These guys came out of thin air and approached us with an offer, and we feel like we have to consider it. Honestly, I'm not surprised it happened; people are starting to get word that we're not quite humming the way we used to. You know how these large agencies are when they smell blood in the water. Agencies are always being acquired—it's the nature of the beast."

He wasn't wrong. Yes, our marketing agency had been struggling. And yes, our industry was second only to Hannibal Lector in how frequently it resorted to cannibalization. It seemed like one agency was gobbling up another on a weekly basis.

But still.

"So, let me see if I have this right. You were approached by a company that wants to acquire us, and you agreed to sign an NDA that restricted me from knowing who it was. That didn't seem like a red flag?"

Several of them looked down at the table, and I could tell this was a sore subject between them. Likely they had debated whether or not to sign something that excluded me from being part of the process. I wondered who was on my side?

Samantha spoke up next. "We didn't want to have to do that, and we knew it was wrong. It was the only way they'd share the offer with us." She turned to James and said, "Are we sure we can't get them to change that part of the agreement?"

"We tried. Samantha, you know we tried. Plus, we barely know much about the company as it is. Remember, they're somewhat secretive with us as well. At this point we are where we are," he said.

"And where exactly are we, James?" I asked, emphasizing the word *we* through gritted teeth.

He began saying something about "due process" and I once again tuned him out. What the hell was happening? I started to wonder if this was some kind of joke...but no, this group of people had many talents, but planning an elaborate prank would not be one of them.

Would this have happened a year ago, when we were growing faster than all the other agencies in town? We had such momentum back then; I couldn't imagine they would have entertained conversations like this during that time. And it was true that we were a little off our game, and sure, we weren't growing as fast, but we were still growing. I had plans to get things back on track, and had even discussed some ideas with Charles last week. I knew there were problems, but I also knew I could fix them. Maybe then they'd see that this was a mistake...and then it hit me.

I just needed time.

James was midway through a statement about some kind of larger economic trend when, apropos of nothing, I blurted out, "Give me six months!"

He stopped what he was saying and the entire board looked at me.

"Sorry, what?" he asked.

"Give me six months. It's true we've had some unexpected turnover and our numbers are a little softer than we had hoped. And I know I've complained a little about my relationship with Paul to a few of you. But all of those things can be fixed. Give me six months to prove to you that this is the worst possible time for us to sell. I promise you won't regret it."

There was silence around the table. The group clearly wasn't expecting this kind of response from me.

"How about giving us a half hour to discuss it?" James asked. "If you can give us the room, we will talk it out and see what we can do."

"You bet," I said. At this point, I'd take what I could get.

As I stood up, I realized that the projector was still presenting on the screen:

Q1 Board Meeting

Let's do this!

I hadn't even made it past the first slide, and my enthusiastic opening made me feel silly.

I turned off the projector, grabbed my laptop, and said, "I'll be right outside."

CHAPTER 2

Our agency was located in the western half of the 17th floor in a high-rise downtown. We moved in a year prior and I still found myself getting lost in the terrific views it provided.

The lobby outside the conference room was one of my favorite spots in the office. It was part of the main thoroughfare: we had purposefully architected the office layout so that people had to pass through it to get from one end of the floor to the other. I was a big believer in serendipitous interactions—the idea that people spending time together (quasi-forced or not) would result in good things.

I plopped myself down on one of the big, comfy chairs. The clock on the wall showed 10:12 a.m. The meeting was meant to run from 10 to 12:30, with lunch brought in around 11:30. I hadn't even made it 15 minutes before finding myself on the wrong side of the conference room door.

I shot Paul a quick text: *You won't believe what just happened.* Let me know when you can talk. Normally he would have been with me in the meeting, but he was on vacation with his family. In fact, ever since we co-founded the company we'd always run the board meetings together. He was going to flip when he heard this news.

I was only alone for a moment before Tina came walking in. She was our office manager and worked at the front desk, which was connected to the lobby. Her desk faced the entrance to our office, opening into the elevator bank. She was the first line of defense for any visitor.

It took her a moment to realize I was sitting there. Upon seeing me she said, "Oh, Will, what are you doing out here? Is everything alright?"

"Yeah. Well, no, actually... I don't know," I said, not ready for the question. "The board just needed a few minutes to chat about some things."

She furrowed her brow. "And they didn't need you to do that?"

I shrugged. "Apparently not."

"Ok, well let me know if I can do anything for you. I checked with the restaurant, and lunch should be arriving around 11:15. I'll get it all set up when it gets here," she said.

"Perfect, thanks."

Steve came bustling around the corner, spotted me, pivoted in my direction, and sat down in the chair next to me. "Hey, boss, what's up?"

Steve was one of the first people I hired after Paul and I started the firm three years ago. Before he joined, I knew Steve by reputation only, but it didn't take long for me to realize he was the guy I wanted to manage our client relationships.

We were in the business of digital advertising and marketing, what most would call a "digital agency." For the most part, we built digital experiences for our clients, with websites, mobile applications, email marketing, and brand messaging making up the core components.

And it didn't matter how well we built something; if we weren't able to forge a good relationship with our customer, then the project would go badly. And that's where Steve shined.

"Nothing much," I said. "Actually, let me ask you a question. Who are the larger agencies in the area that might be in the acquisition game, looking to acquire shops our size?"

"Why, is there something…"

"No, not at all, I was just curious. I've been reading that there might be some M&A activity coming up in our space and thought I'd start game-planning in case shops start merging." It wasn't a lie, exactly. I had read something like that.

"Huh, lemme think for a second," he said. "The way I see it there are probably only a few that would fit the bill. Massive and Codeword 9 come to mind. They're big and have acquired a few smaller shops in the last few years."

"Right, and the only other one I can think of is Brainstick. I don't know if they've acquired any agencies, but they're big enough and seem to have a lot of momentum," I said.

"Right, forgot about them. How do these agencies come up with their names? Anyway, those are the only three I can think of. I gotta get back out there, these clients aren't going to manage themselves," he said with a laugh.

As Steve walked out, I received a text back from Paul:

hey, i know i'm in a different time zone, but aren't you still supposed to be in the board meeting? can't wait to hear what's going on but we're about to do some snorkeling. ping you later.

I fired back a quick reply, *Sounds good, talk later.*

I stood up and said, "Hey Tina, will you let me know when the Board asks for me? I'm going to head to my office and get some work done until then."

"You bet," she said.

As I made my way down the hall, I was quickly reminded of the success we experienced just a few years back. Along the wall, we had set up the business awards we had won, mainly so that visiting clients, prospects, and potential new employees would see that we were a legit agency.

The awards ranged from Most Engaging Marketing Campaign to Best Places to Work. Some were for specific campaigns we had produced for clients, others for our fast growth and great culture. But as I made my way past them, they didn't feel as relevant today. In fact, at the last awards show, we had come up surprisingly empty—the first time that had ever happened.

We blamed it on a lot of things. That client wouldn't let us run the campaign we wanted to run, this award submission wasn't as crisp as it could have been, that judge didn't like us (someone actually said that)—but I knew there was something more going on. I just hadn't been able to put my finger on it.

Turning a corner, I entered what we affectionately called, "The Farm." The Farm was essentially a large high-walled cubicle farm where most of the agency worked. The executives and I had offices along the outer edges of the floor, which, of course, included the windows with the dazzling views.

I rounded the final turn and entered my office, closed the door, and sat down in my chair. One thing we had invested in when we moved into this building were nice chairs for everyone. A team member showed me research proving that ergonomic chairs, along with a second monitor, are the best investments you can make for your team members. So we splurged, and now everyone sits comfortably while they look at their dual monitors. We didn't really notice a spike in productivity, but it looked super cool, so from an ROI perspective, we had that going for us.

Personally, I had zero monitors on my desk. I was a laptop-only kinda guy. My laptop went everywhere with me, and I didn't like a lot of clutter, so my desk was almost completely empty. The one consistent thing on my desk was the photo of Sarah, Danielle, and me on vacation from last summer. Danielle was just over a year old in the shot, as evidenced by her blurry left arm, as no doubt she wiggled and squirmed while the picture was taken.

I set my laptop down on the desk, opened it up, and started scanning my email. But my eyes could barely focus on the screen. My mind kept coming back to one question.

What was I going to do?

"Will, did you hear me? The board is ready for you now."

Tina had poked her head into my office and was gesturing at me to come with her. Shaking myself back into reality, I grabbed my laptop and followed her back to the conference room.

"What time is it?" I asked her as we made our way to the lobby.

"11:15," she said.

They had deliberated for an hour; was that a good sign or a bad sign?

I took a deep breath and entered the conference room.

CHAPTER 3

"So what happened next?" Paul asked.

Paul and I had finally connected on a call later that afternoon. After hearing about his snorkeling adventures for as long as I could bear, I nearly exploded with the news of what had happened with the board.

"Well, after waiting almost an hour, I entered the board room and man, were they tense. No one said anything as I made my way to my seat. I think I made a bad joke, but honestly, I can't remember. Maybe I said nothing. Either way, James kicked things off by telling me that they had considered my request, and the first thing they wanted to know was whether or not I had a plan for the next six months."

"And, do you have a plan?" he asked.

"You mean, do *we* have a plan, right? We're in this together, bucko. And that was actually what I told them. That I had some ideas, but you and I would have to spend time formulating a plan, and I wouldn't dream of doing that without you next to me. I did reassure them that it could be done, and that they wouldn't regret giving us the time to get back on track."

Continuing, I said, "Then they agreed…kinda. They said the acquisition process would take about six months anyway, so there was no harm in continuing down that road while also letting us work on fixing the business. I tried to get them to pause for six months, pointing out that continuing the acquisition process would be very distracting, but they said that was the best they could do."

"Do you believe, even if we end up making some big improvements over the next six months, that they'd walk away from a great deal?" he asked.

"I guess I have to at this point. I also want to figure out who is behind this. Best I can figure, it's either Brainstick, Codeword 9, or Massive," I said.

Paul was silent for a moment, then said, "Yeah, I can't think of any other firms that would be able to do a deal like this, at least not locally."

"So on that front, I'm going to work on setting up meetings with the CEOs of those companies to see if I can figure out who's behind this," I said.

"What good will that do?"

"I've always believed that if you know your competition, you know how to fight them. I believe it was Sun Tzu that said, 'Know thy enemy and know yourself; in a hundred battles you will never be in peril.'"

"Oh no, you're quoting *The Art of War*, I know this is getting serious," he said, laughing. "Okay, I gotta go. Anything you need me to do before I get back next week? Happy to jump in if needed."

"Nope, have fun and get some rest. You'll need it—this is going to be a lot of work," I said.

We hung up. I really appreciated having Paul as a partner. He was always game to roll up his sleeves and get to work.

Our relationship had started five years earlier, back when I was at Crackersnap. Paul was running operations for a software company we partnered with, and we got to know each other over a series of meetings.

We quickly found that we had a lot in common, including an interest in entrepreneurship. Both of us were working at a startup, and we both wanted to experience what it would be like to start our own thing.

We also began to realize that we had different skill sets and passions, which we believed would be a great match for a business partnership. I was more vision and growth-oriented, and he was more operations and process-focused. The more we talked, the more we realized that this was something we might be able to do together.

As with most startups, the first year was tough. It didn't help that neither of us had built a business before. We both put what little money we had into the business, and it took us almost 12 months to finally start to see progress.

Starting a business is tough both professionally and personally. Sarah and I had married several years prior, and those early days were not easy on our relationship. I was working around the clock and not drawing a paycheck.

With our savings running out and no clear path to generating significant revenue in the business, Sarah and I made the hard decision to move in with her parents. I think she was against it more than I was, but we really had no other choice. She brought it up first.

"I don't know how we can afford to keep living in this apartment once our lease is up next month," she said. We were in a very small apartment in what should have been a very affordable area of town. Should being the operative word.

"I know. The business is so close on a few sales opportunities. Maybe a few will hit before we have to decide…," I trailed off, not even believing what I was selling. It wasn't that I didn't believe in the business, but we just needed more time, and I saw no real path to any sudden, quick wins in our future.

"I believe in you, you know that, right?" she asked, putting her hand on my shoulder. I nodded my head. "So why don't we take a little pressure off and give you more 'runway,' as you call it. I think maybe... we should move in with my parents."

"What? No way! There must be another option. I'm not even sure your dad likes me yet!"

"Come on, I'm pretty certain you're one of his favorite son-in-laws," she said with a wry smile.

I laughed because I was, in fact, his only son-in-law.

"You know he loves you, and even if he didn't, what other options do we have? If we stay with them for, let's say a year, we can give you the time you need. As soon as we're ready, we'll move out, I promise. And you wouldn't have to feel so guilty about working late," she said.

It all made sense, of course. And I could tell this was the last thing she wanted to do. I had put us in this mess, and I would have to swallow my pride and do what was best for the family. But I desperately did not want her parents to think I could not support my family. Maybe we could position it to her parents as something we didn't need to do, but rather wanted to be able to invest in the business more. That would at least save my ego from having to take as much of a hit.

"Do you think your parents would even have us?" I asked.

"Actually," she said, looking up at me. "It was their idea."

Great, so much for the old misdirection, save-the-ego scheme.

Throughout that next year, we did start to hit our stride as a business. As things improved, we were able to move back into our own apartment, and soon after that our daughter, Danielle, was born.

Paul and I continued to make a good team, though we came from different schools of thought on many things. The biggest disagreements centered on how we wanted to grow and ultimately, what our end game was with the business. Paul had, from the very start, been focused on building in order to sell. As we batted around decisions, he always leaned toward the ones that would give us the best chance to position the company for a sale. It wasn't that I was against that, but over time, I became a little more interested in the idea of building something for the long term.

One of our biggest disagreements happened when we discussed the idea of open-book management. I had read an article about the concept, whereby a company shared their finances openly with all team members, with the idea being to build trust and increase problem-solving across the entire company.

Paul was against it from the start.

"You know how our numbers shift constantly, and how we have very little visibility into the future! The team would freak out if they saw those things," he said.

He was right about the inability to see too far into the future. The nature of our business was project-based, with those projects typically lasting for three to six months. We did not have many long-term, retainer-based relationships that would allow us to project revenue over an entire year. A less-informed individual might see our financials and think we'd be going out of business in six months.

"Yes, there's a chance of that, but think of the upside! We'd have team members that would help us problem-solve and they'd feel more invested in the business. Plus, the long-term trust we would earn by sharing this with the team would be invaluable," I said, pleading my case.

It was true that as CEO I could technically force this decision through, but I had decided from the beginning that if Paul and

I didn't agree on a big move, we wouldn't do it. It allowed, in my mind, for a checks-and-balances style of decision-making.

"Will, if we're hoping to sell the business in the next few years, it doesn't really matter that we build long-term trust with the team, right? You know as well as I, once we sell, we're likely only going to be around for a few months to transition, then we're gone. Why would we rock the boat if that's the plan?"

It was these kinds of conversations that frustrated me, partly because he was right. If our plan was to sell in the next few years, then we wouldn't make a lot of big moves that focused on culture, but would rather focus specifically on revenue growth and bottom-line profit. And so I would relent, not yet ready to share my feelings that maybe, just maybe, we should build this company into something special; something that would last even beyond the two of us.

Will and his team did ultimately implement open-book management several years later, and you can read about that in Book 3 of *The Turnaround Leadership Series: The Great Team Turnaround.*

And so it went. I would have some kind of big—often what you might call hair-brained—idea, and Paul would steer the conversation back to the idea of us selling the business. That was until several months earlier when I summoned the courage to bring up the idea of building our business for the long term. He was justifiably upset when I suggested that.

"Will, what are you talking about? We've been saying we want to sell the business since the beginning!"

"Actually, you've been saying that. I've never been fully on board…"

He cut me off. "How can you say that? You never corrected me when I brought up the idea of selling!"

"I know, that's true and I should have. But I haven't always thought this way; it's just that the more I think about what this business could be, and honestly, the good we could do in the world with it, the more I think maybe we should think about our goals a bit differently."

"I can't believe this is happening," he said, almost talking to himself now. "I've maxed out several credit cards, mortgaged my house, all because I thought we were going to sell, and now you're suggesting we don't sell? How am I supposed to accept that?"

I was aware he was in a worse financial situation than myself, but apparently I wasn't aware of just how dire it was. "Don't worry, we'll figure it out, and I'm not saying we won't sell, I'm just saying…"

We continued to go round and round, both raising our voices at times, until I finally had to leave for a meeting.

I felt terrible, mostly because he was right. I had been the dishonest one, and I was the one suggesting we change our plans for the business.

For weeks after that we seemed "off." Avoiding each other when we could, being matter-of-fact when we did have to communicate. I was pretty sure the only way we'd be able to move on was if we had another shouting match, but I was hesitant to set it up. I hated fighting with him.

Finally, after a few weeks and as things normally do after time passes, we seemed to return to normal. I was surprised early one morning when he texted me:

hey, sorry i got upset a few weeks ago. i understand people and companies change over time. are we good?

Relieved, I quickly texted back:

You bet, and sorry I wasn't more honest before about my change of heart. Let's find time soon to grab dinner and discuss.

After a few minutes he replied with a simple:

great

I'd take it. And while we hadn't found the time to grab that dinner, we were starting to jive again. And the timing couldn't have been better for us to get back on track, because I wasn't sure I could go through this hostile takeover (which is what I was calling it now, emphasis on the hostile) without him by my side. I was certain he'd be critical in figuring out what was going on and how to get back on track.

I just had no idea how critical.

MONTH 1

CHAPTER 4

It was 5:45 on Monday morning as I entered the elevator in our building. I spent the weekend having a hard time thinking about anything other than the challenge that lay ahead of me.

Sarah had been patient with me over the weekend, but even she could take only so much. We spent most of Sunday at the park, and at one point she was pushing Danielle on the swing while I stood next to her, lost in thought.

"Earth to Mr. Businessman," she said, waving her hands in front of my face.

Laughing, I said, "Sorry, I must have zoned out there a bit."

"A bit? More like all weekend. I know you have a lot on your mind, but remember we're here, too."

"I'm sorry, you're right," I said. Staying present with Sarah and Danielle was something I was working to be better at. Without question, they were the most important things in my life. Challenges at work could seem like the most important things to focus on, but I always regretted it when I chose to spend time (and mental energy) on my business rather than on them.

"Well, I can see that you aren't likely to be able to find your way back to us until you have some kind of decision made, so maybe I can help. What's your biggest concern?"

"I think it's that I don't have the foggiest idea of how to get started.

Over the next six months I have to recharge the business so that it starts performing significantly better than it has been, and so much better that the board has no other choice but to bow out of the acquisition deal that's on the table. And while I'm not even sure that's possible, I know it won't happen if I can't even figure out how to get started!"

"Well, other than you, who would know?"

I thought about that for a moment. "Well, perhaps Paul, but I think he's as clueless as I am…I suppose the leadership team?"

"Then maybe that's where you start," she said. Danielle jumped off the swing and made her way over to the jungle gym.

As we walked that way, I said, "The problem is that I can't tell the leadership team what's really going on. Due to the NDA that the board signed, I have to keep silent about it. In fact, you're not even supposed to know."

"Oh shoot, well I just posted about it on Facebook, let me see if I can delete my message," she said, grabbing her phone and pretending to use it.

"Ha ha, very funny. But seriously, how can I talk to the leadership team without spilling the beans?" I asked.

"Do you believe there's a problem with the business?" she asked.

"I do now. Ever since that board meeting, I've started to look at the company through a new lens, and there are more problems than I realized."

"Then why not start there? You can simply say you've been spending time thinking about the business and you feel like things are 'off,' and then ask them if they feel the same way. I bet you'll be surprised how much they agree," she said. Then she added, "That is, if you can get them to be honest with you."

"What's that supposed to mean?" I asked, not hiding my unhappiness with the suggestion. "You don't think they're honest with me?"

"Look, Will," she said, "I think in most companies, people find it hard to disagree with the boss. Telling the person who signs your paycheck that their baby is ugly isn't the easiest thing to do. And then you add in your obvious passion for the company...yeah, I think there's a chance that they hold back a little when sharing their thoughts. But maybe I'm wrong and they'll come right out with it when you talk to them."

I thought about that and decided I would make a special effort when I met with the leadership team to get them to tell me the truth. They already did that, I was sure of it. Right? How would I know? Did I not give them the impression that I wanted honesty from them above all else? What if they always held back a little?

Just then, Sarah waved her hands in front of my face again.

"Okay, now that you have a plan, can we get back to being a family for the rest of the weekend?"

"Absolutely. Let's take Danielle to the ice cream shop. I've had my eye on that new cappuccino flavor they just added." And with that, we scooped up our daughter and headed for the car.

CHAPTER 5

Sarah had of course been right about talking to the team, which is why I got in particularly early to the office today. I needed time to get my head in the right place, and I always find that I do my best thinking early in the morning, in the quiet before everyone starts arriving.

Using my badge to enter, I made my way to my office, flipping light switches along the way. I put my laptop down on my desk and circled my way to the kitchen area where I started brewing a pot of coffee.

Paul and I would meet at 8:30 to start formulating our plan. Then at 10 we would have our weekly leadership team meeting, which we would use to start digging into the health of our company. And then later today I had a meeting with my mentor, Charles. Boy did I need that meeting.

It would be a busy day, for sure, but busyness always helps to calm my nerves. We had six months to make this happen, and it started today.

At 8:30 on the dot, my phone vibrated. I picked it up and the message read:

running a few minutes late, kid decided to forget one of his shoes which we didn't realize until we were halfway to daycare

Paul and his wife were juggling quite a bit. Both of them worked in entrepreneurial jobs, and that sometimes resulted in situations like this that were out of his control. And in this specific case, I knew his pain, as I had once dropped Danielle off at a playdate without either of her shoes. I still hear about that from Sarah.

"Hey, Will, got a second?" Steve asked, poking his head through the open door to my office.

"Actually, I do now. Come on in," I said.

Steve entered and sat down in the chair across from my desk. He was one of the most positive people I knew, which is part of what makes him a great account leader. His upbeat personality was infectious, and I was glad he had come to see me—I could use some of that positive energy this morning.

He smiled and said, "I have some good news about RedBrick."

RedBrick was one of our earliest customers, and had grown nicely over the last few years. Like most clients, we had started with a small assignment, a medium-sized website build for one of their divisions. Our plan as a company was always to do whatever we could to start working with a client and then over-deliver on the work while being a kind, thoughtful, and attentive partner. If we did those two things, we almost always saw growth with the customer.

That was exactly what happened with RedBrick. That first project led to two more, and we were now close to being their only digital marketing partner.

"That's great, what's the latest?" I asked.

"As you know, I found out a few weeks ago that they are only working with one other agency, and it sounds like soon they might have a jump ball for their entire relationship!"

"A jump ball?" I asked.

"Oh, sorry, that's a term we used at my last job. It means that they would put us up against the other agency they work with, Massive, and give us some kind of assignment or pitch to see who wins. And the winner gets the whole enchilada! We could put ourselves in a position to win all of their work!"

That would be huge. Of course, we could also lose everything, but I wasn't going to remind Steve of that.

"That's fantastic, and what a testament to the team and your leadership. Just the chance to knock a shop like Massive off this account would be exciting. When do you think you'll know if they're going to do it?" I asked.

"We have a meeting next month where I expect to learn more, but I doubt it will be in this quarter. They'll probably want to have the decision line up with their new fiscal year, which is in about six months," he said.

Big sales pitches like this typically take three to four months, which means they'd likely start in a few months.

"Okay, knowing this ahead of time is excellent; it allows us to begin prepping the team well ahead of the game. I can also make sure to connect with Mark over the next month just to keep the relationship tight from the top," I said.

Mark was the CMO, or Chief Marketing Officer, of RedBrick. For our largest and most important accounts, I always made sure to have a good relationship with the top leader. In almost all cases that would mean the CMO, as they are responsible for all marketing initiatives for the company.

"Perfect," he said as he made his way toward the door to my office. "There's nothing like a big winner-takes-all competition to get people excited around here again!"

As Steve left my office, I thought to myself: "People need to get excited around here again?"

Almost as soon as Steve left, Paul entered my office. He closed the door and made his way to the couch along the far wall. I grabbed my notepad and walked over to join him, sitting in one of the chairs that faced the couch.

"Rough morning?" I asked.

"Same old, same old," he said. "I wish I could say this was the first time I left the house with a one-shoed kid. Not my proudest moment as a father, I can tell you that. Hey, didn't you do that once at a playdate or something?"

Laughing, I said, "Yeah, don't remind me. Also, once I went shopping and was so intent on getting the right size and type of diapers for Danielle—there are seemingly thousands of combinations, those sections of the grocery store should come with a how-to manual—that I came home with a box of Big Boy Diapers. You would have thought the blue color would have tipped me off."

"Actually I remember that. She had to wear those for about a month, right?"

"Yeah, I thought I was being thrifty by getting the surplus-sized box," I said, smiling at the memory.

We both took a sip of coffee, and I kicked things off. I always started meetings by stating the goal of what we hoped to accomplish. I read somewhere that meetings are exponentially more effective if there's an agreed-upon goal, and that's proved true ever since I started doing it.

"We have a little under six months to prove to the board that the business has far too much potential to sell right now," I said. "And more to the point, we have two months before the next board meeting, which means we need to have both a plan and some progress against it."

"So they want to meet every two months at this point?" he asked.

Typically we held our board meetings quarterly, but given the six-month timeline, we agreed that we'd meet more frequently to provide updates and progress.

"Right, which means we have two more board meetings before

the big one, where hopefully they'll be so wowed by our progress that they'll forgo any thoughts of selling the business."

Paul shifted in his seat a bit. He said, "And you think there's something wrong with the business right now?"

"I do. I don't know what it is, exactly, but I know you can feel it, too. A year ago we were firing on all cylinders. We were winning new business faster than we could staff it, the awards were piling up, and people were banging down our door trying to get a job with us. And there was an energy around the place that...well, felt different than it does now."

I thought about what Steve had said just moments earlier, how people needed to get excited around here...

"I don't really see it, but I'll take your word for it. And you mentioned something in your note to me about wanting to ask the leadership team? You know we can't let them know about the sale process."

"Just the fact that you and I can't see what's happening around here shows me that we need their help. I think we can couch the conversation as a bit of a SWOT analysis. Get them talking about the things we're doing well, and then move into areas of opportunities and threats. That way, it's part of a standard business analysis," I said.

We had run SWOT (Strengths, Weaknesses, Opportunities, and Threats) analyses before. While the end result is always helpful, I found the actual process of analyzing the business extremely insightful. People start sharing their real feelings about the business, which can, as Sarah pointed out, sometimes be hard to say to their managers.

"That could work, I suppose," he said. "So then we'll take the results of the SWOT and come up with a plan?"

"Yes. I'm also meeting up with Charles this afternoon. I think he'll be able to help me see through the fog a bit. After that, we can come up with our plan."

We spent a few more minutes getting ready for the leadership team meeting. With five minutes remaining before the meeting start time, Paul grabbed his stuff and went to go refill his coffee. I walked to the door of my office and looked out at the team.

The dress code at our company could best be described as: *relaxed.* You could fairly easily determine the roles people played at the agency by their attire. The creatives and developers typically dressed in jeans and T-shirts, or depending on the time of year, jeans and hoodies. Lots of tattoos and indiscriminate piercings, and hair that appeared as if it hadn't been combed in weeks. They enjoyed their freedom and I was all for it.

Project managers and operation team members were dressed in alignment with their detail-oriented roles. The men wore khakis and button-downs, with loafers and matching belts, while the women wore stylish but conservative dresses or...khakis and button-downs.

The sales and account leaders—those that were constantly meeting with clients or attending events, and always focused on growth—were the most stylish of the group. Dress shirts, slacks, and dresses were not out of the ordinary but were usually reserved for specific events. On an average day, if you caught a handful of them together and snapped a photo, it could be the cover of a Banana Republic brochure.

I was somewhere in the middle, preferring designer jeans and a company t-shirt when I could get away with it, opting for expensive sneakers that weren't too obnoxious, and yes, I did comb my hair. (I was convinced the creatives did in fact comb and style their hair to look messy, but to date, I had no definitive proof.)

When it came time for a big meeting I would put on a nice button-down shirt, but usually kept the jeans and sneakers. I convinced myself that clients wanted the CEO of their agency to have at least a twinge of creativity in them, but really, I just felt more comfortable dressing casually.

Currently, there were a lot of people at their desks, working quietly with their dual monitors and fancy chairs. I tried to picture what this scene would have looked like even six months prior. I remember once giving a client a tour of our office around this time of day, and as we made our way back to my office, she commented on how charged up she was from the energy and passion she had experienced in those few minutes. She said, "I've never seen a group of people so excited about their jobs! I don't know how you did that, but it's something I hope you never take for granted."

Looking around again at everyone silently pecking away at their keyboards, I couldn't help but think that we had.

CHAPTER 6

The Leadership Team meeting was always one of my favorite times of the week. It was my chance to regroup with the top leaders in the company, hear the latest progress, and most importantly, see how I could help. Today, however, I needed their help.

"Good morning! How was your weekend?" I asked Rachel, the only member of the team in the conference room so far. I made a quick glance at the clock on the wall. 9:58 a.m. The rest of the team still had a few minutes to get here; one thing I did not tolerate was lateness to meetings.

Rachel was our Head of Operations. At a marketing agency like ours, operations was one of the most critical areas. Her job entails making sure that the work we do for clients is delivered on point, on time, and on budget. She is also responsible for everything that goes into allowing that work to happen: equipment, tools, processes, and even the right team members. She works hand in hand with Martha, our Head of HR, to make sure we are staffed appropriately for the work we have.

"Great," she replied. "We finally finished building the garden in the backyard. We were only a few days off from our project plan for the job, which is good because I don't think Jim could have handled any more of my micro-management."

"Well, tell him he can join the emotional support group I formed when we first started working together," I said. She rolled her eyes and we both laughed. Her ability to wrangle me, and apparently her husband, to get the job done was second to none. And although I liked to kid her from time to time, I couldn't imagine working without her on the team.

Ahmet and Martha came in at the same time. Ahmet was the Head of Business Development for the firm, which meant his main role was to bring in new clients. He and Steve worked together on big initiatives, but while Steve was focused on nurturing and growing our existing relationships, Ahmet was always on the hunt for the next new partner.

As they grabbed their seats, Ahmet said, "Rachel, I saw the pics of your new garden on Instagram—it looks amazing! Happy with how it turned out?"

"You bet, and mostly happy that we finished it on budget, and almost on time," she said, giving me a wink.

Steve and Paul entered next, right as the clock struck 10.

"Welcome everyone," I said. "Let's get rolling, because there's an exercise I want us to go through toward the end of the meeting. Who wants to start?"

It was my process to encourage people to speak up at these meetings, which I felt allowed for the most important items to bubble up for discussion. I tried having a formal agenda in the past, but it always seemed to result in stale, "Let's just get through this," kind of meetings. Actually, my current process for running these meetings didn't help much with that problem—perhaps all meetings were destined to be mostly boring—but at least I didn't have to create an agenda any longer.

"I'll go first," Steve said. "I was telling Will this earlier, but I have reason to believe that RedBrick will be throwing up a jump ball between us and the other agency they work with soon. It appears they want to consolidate to just one agency. I'll keep you all up to date as I learn more, but I expect it to be a few months from now."

"Which means we need to make sure we're over-delivering on the account from this point forward," I said.

Ahmet spoke up next. "Steve, let me know how I can help when we do get the invitation to pitch. We've been working on some new ways to make pitches exciting."

"Sure thing," said Steve.

Martha raised her hand. She did this from time to time, which fit her personality. She was the quietest and most introverted member of the leadership team, and she was also the most thoughtful and empathetic. Which made her perfect to oversee Human Resources.

After telling her she could go next (and reminding her that she didn't have to raise her hand in these meetings) she said, "I think we need to discuss the recent turnover we've had. I have a one-pager to walk you all through."

She pulled out a stack of papers—she always had handouts—and passed around a page to each of us. At the top it read:

Turnover: The Secret Killer

"Is this a one-pager or the synopsis of a thriller you're writing?" Steve asked.

"Oh, I assure you, it's much scarier than anything I could come up with on my own," Martha replied.

Looking over the very detailed (and immaculately formatted) document, I said, "Wait, this can't be right. It says over the last six months our turnover has doubled, from less than 5% to just over 10%! Are you sure this data is accurate?"

"It's definitely accurate; I re-ran the numbers a few times to be sure. I'm a little surprised that you hadn't noticed. Many of the people who've left recently sat right outside your office in The Farm," Martha said.

"I knew we lost some good folks to some of the larger firms, but I didn't realize it was that high," I said. How had I not noticed? Come to think of it, I *had* been spending more time in my office lately in closed-door meetings.

Rachel said, "The important thing is that we're aware now. Can you take us through the document so we get the full picture? I'm particularly interested in the reasons that people gave for leaving."

For the next 15 minutes, Martha took us through the report, and the news was not good. Most of the people who left mentioned in the exit interview that they felt like our agency had changed, using phrases like "feels too corporate now" and "leadership is disconnected." Ouch.

When we were finished, I said, "Thank you for that sobering look at our turnover, Martha. This leads into the larger conversation I want to have with you all this morning. Paul and I think it would be a good use of our time to start thinking through a mini-SWOT analysis on the business. Given the data we just looked at, the fact that we won a total of zero awards at the last award show, and the slower rate at which we're growing, it is clear that something has changed in the business. I know that you are all feeling this in various ways, and I'd like us to be open and honest about what you think is happening."

I looked around the room at the team, and with no one willing to get the ball rolling, I said, "Paul, why don't you start with what you think might be happening."

"Sure," he said. "Rachel and I have been talking about the fact that our growth has slowed and the increased financial burden we've seen in our expenses because of that."

Paul, as our COO and President, oversaw all of our operations and finance. This was where his great strengths so perfectly complemented mine. Rachel reported directly to him and the two worked very closely together.

Rachel added, "I've been studying agency trends recently, and it seems that with slower growth, profit margins naturally drop while at the same time turnover does typically increase, causing the need to spend more time and money hiring new team members. It also becomes more expensive to hire those new team members when morale is low, thus further increasing costs."

"And when our profit drops," Ahmet said, jumping in, "we are unwilling to spend as much on marketing and sales, which makes it harder for us to start growing again."

"Culture takes a big hit when we stop growing as well," Martha said.

Steve said, "And when culture is low, our team's performance drops, and clients are unhappy, resulting in…"

"Less growth," Rachel said, "which starts the entire process over again."

I stood up and walked to the whiteboard. There was a trend I heard in their comments that I wanted to explore.

"So let me see if I have this right. We have seemingly many problems right now, all of which are connected. One huge issue at the moment is that we're not winning enough new business," I said.

I wrote *Winning less new business* on the whiteboard.

"What else?" I asked.

"Turnover is up," said Martha.

"Our work is subpar," said Steve, "and clients are unhappy."

Rachel said, "Our expenses have increased because of all of this."

"Which has resulted in a drop in profit," Paul added.

I wrote all of those things on the board, with a big empty circle in the middle that connected them all.

"I think those are the big issues we've identified. And it occurs to me that there is one common denominator that they all have in common, and which affects all of them. Anyone have an idea of what that is?" I asked.

They thought for a moment, looking at what I had written on the whiteboard.

"It's culture," Rachel said. "When our culture suffers, our work suffers. Clients are unhappy, and turnover increases. We win less business when our team is unhappy, and our profits drop due to the lack of growth and the increased expenses to hire new team members."

"And new team members come into a broken culture and are allowed to act in ways we never would have allowed before, thus continuing to create a poor culture," said Steve.

"Exactly!" I said, and wrote *Culture* in the middle. "Culture affects every one of these problems, and every one of these problems affects culture."

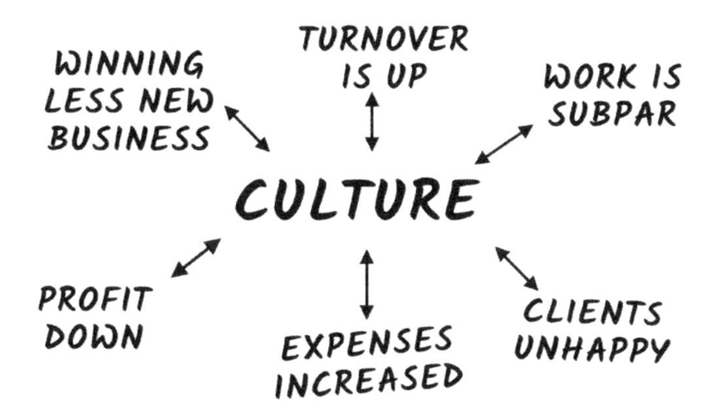

Checking my watch, I said, "We're out of time for this meeting, but I think this is good work. I appreciate you all talking so openly about our problems, but I also wish you had done so earlier. I hope you know you can be honest with me about the business; in fact, that's the only way we'll build the company we want to build. And I need to do a better job being aware of what's happening in the company. That's on me."

After the team left, I turned my chair around and looked at the whiteboard. Ok, now I see the problem...but what do I do about it?

"Will, over here!"

I looked across the expanse of the park, past a couple throwing a frisbee and a family having a picnic, and saw Charles waving vigorously to me. Charles had a way of doing everything... vigorously.

I met Charles the previous year when we were both part of a citywide brand campaign. Charles impressed me during that meeting, and I set out to make him my mentor. Luckily, he agreed to take me on, and we'd been meeting consistently each month.

As I approached Charles, I could see that he had biked to the park. He was likely in his mid-50s, and was the most active person I ever met. He once told me that in his early years he was out of shape and generally lazy—which I found hard to believe but he assured me was the truth—and at some point he had a "health awakening" that led him to take his health much more seriously.

Case in point: Charles always insisted that we meet outside, and often while doing something active. So it was no surprise when he suggested we meet at the large park in our area. Foothills Park had long been my favorite place to meet up in the city.

"Will, have a seat and watch what these kids can do," he said as I joined him on the bench. We were sitting in front of a massive skateboarding complex, with kids of all ages and sizes doing their best Tony Hawk impressions.

Directly in front of us appeared to be the most advanced area, with a huge swimming pool-like bowl complete with three platforms of different sizes and shapes throughout. The bowl itself had a green rim around it, with the actual floor painted a dark red. Each flat surface at the top of the platforms was green, giving the whole place what could only be described as a "Christmas" feel, if it wasn't so dang...cool.

He pointed at a girl who couldn't have been more than 12 years old, and said, "Watch what she can do."

She was navigating her way around the other skaters and, as luck would have it, was coming in our direction with great speed. She accelerated as she hit the beginning of the wall, leaning into the curve and as her skateboard passed the summit of the bowl, she began to spin, her velocity taking her higher than our heads. While in the air she made two full rotations and came down perfectly back into the bowl.

I found myself clapping along with all the other spectators, and I asked Charles, "Was that what people hipper than me would call a 720?"

"Yep," he said, laughing. "And that's the third time she's done that. I think it's no coincidence that she does that in front of the crowd each time."

We continued watching for another 15 minutes, with Charles pointing out a few of the skaters and explaining what they were doing.

"How do you know so much about skateboarding?" I asked.

"It's a relatively new passion for me," he said. Noticing the stunned look on my face, he added, "Oh no, not a passion for actually doing that. At my age, can you imagine? No, a passion for watching. Ever since they built this skateboarding park a few years back, I've been coming up to watch somewhat frequently. A few times people have educated me on the basics."

"Well, I wouldn't put it past you to give it a try. Weren't you recently rock climbing in Nevada?" I asked.

"In Red Rock. Truly great time. I went with a group of adventure buddies and we spent a week up there. But, that's an entirely different ball game than what these kids are doing. I can climb a 200-foot ravine no problem, but ask me to stand on a skateboard and go over the edge of that bowl, I couldn't even imagine it."

"Uh-huh," I said. "Well, both of those things sound equally terrifying to me."

"Let's go for a walk and you can tell me what's going on with the business," he said.

We stood up and entered the path that traversed the park. I began by explaining to Charles what happened at the board meeting. I also reminded him that all of this would be much easier if he would finally agree to be on my board.

He laughed and said, "Actually, it sounds like a tough board to be on! But in all seriousness, and as I've told you, I really do appreciate the offer, but being a casual advisor to you is better for both of us. I don't have to sit in stuffy meetings and be confined to a schedule, and you can ask me anything, at any time, and always get a totally unbiased and honest answer. There's strength in having mentors and advisors that are not financially connected to your business."

"Fair enough, and I'll pretend you didn't just call my board meetings 'stuffy,'" I said with a grin. "So, what do you think?"

"Well, it *is* very unusual to have this happen without your involvement. That is, given what you've told me about the relationship you have with the board. If you were constantly battling the board, and if you had a very different vision for where to take the business than they did, then I could see them working on a sale of the business without involving you. But you've always had a solid relationship with them, correct?"

I nodded and said, "Correct. They've always been very supportive. We've never even had a disagreement of any significance, actually."

"It's also fairly unconventional for the acquiring party to not want to involve the CEO. That can really only mean one thing," he said.

"What's that?" I asked.

"They clearly don't want you involved in the business after the sale. Which is equally odd in your industry. In most cases, a purchaser won't even consider buying a marketing agency without the CEO committed to staying on for a few years. In this case, they don't even want you to know about it. It would appear that they think they can run this without you, and would prefer to, actually," he said.

Wow. I had not even thought about that.

"Why would they think they could run the business without me involved? This is why I need to figure out which company is trying to buy us," I said. "It just makes no sense."

"Hmm," he said. We were winding our way through the area of the park with a lake and were approaching a family of ducks crossing the path. There were eight of them in a line, as ducks often are, but the duck just behind the leader was about a foot over to the right. The rest of the ducks were in line behind the first one.

As we stopped to let them on their way, he said, "I'm not sure what could be going on, but there must be a reason they think they can run the business without you. We can circle back to that. Why do you think the board is even considering this?"

"I think it's a combination of the offer that was made—which I can only assume was generous—and, as we've discussed, the fact that we have been struggling over the last six or so months. In fact, just this morning I had a meeting with the leadership team and they informed me just how much we are off track," I said.

I then shared with Charles how the leadership team meeting went, and the whiteboarding exercise I had taken them through at the end.

"So it's about culture, then?" Charles asked.

"It appears that way to me. What do you think?" I asked.

"In my experience, almost every serious problem a company faces can be linked back to culture. A company's culture is its lifeblood, from which everything can be accomplished. At the same time, a toxic culture can silently suck the life out of a company," he said.

"That's exactly what it feels like," I said. "Each of the problems we've been experiencing have generally been small and annoying, but absorbable, and it wasn't until this morning that I started to see the way that all of these issues are interconnected, with our culture at the center."

"What you need to do, then, is get your culture back on track," Charles said.

"Actually, I'd say we need to build a stronger culture than we ever had before. The reality is, as much as we thought we had a great culture in the past, it clearly wasn't built to create stability over the long term. What we need to build is a…" I paused, searching for the most appropriate word.

"An **undeniable** culture!" Charles said. "You need a culture that is built on core truths—one that is so deeply woven into the fabric of your business that it takes on a life of its own and grows into something truly magical."

"An *undeniable* culture…that sounds incredible!" I said. "So, how do I do *that*?"

We were rounding the north end of the lake as the sun was rising over the tree line surrounding the park. I noticed the ducks we had let pass earlier were already a good distance into the lake, still in a single file line, except for the second duck who was still just off center.

"Well, the *how* of it is a bit trickier. Let's pause on that for now. You said you were going to try to figure out which company was making the offer to buy your business?" he asked.

"Yeah, as far as I can tell, there are three potential acquirers. My plan is to meet with their CEOs and see if I can sniff out which of them is making the offer," I said.

"I'm always a fan of getting to know the competition, and in this case, I think it's an exceptionally smart idea to attempt to figure out who is looking to acquire you. Perhaps while you're meeting with them and learning about their businesses, you'll learn more about how they've built their cultures—the good and the bad—and it will give you ideas on how to shape your culture turnaround," he said.

"That's a great idea," I said. We kept chatting for a few more minutes and eventually ended up at the bike rack. Charles unlocked his bike, put on his helmet, and rejoined me on the path.

Walking his bike next to me as we headed to the park exit, Charles said, "One more thing, Will. As you go on this journey, pay attention to everything. Open your mind's aperture and take in as much as you can. Look at everything and everyone through a new lens. This will likely be the biggest challenge you've been through with your business, and you don't want to miss a thing."

I thanked him for the advice and he jumped on his bike and was off.

Making my way back to where I parked, I thought about what he just said.

"Open your mind's aperture."

"Look at everything and everyone through a new lens."

Did Charles think I was missing something obvious?

CHAPTER 7

"An undeniable culture, huh?"

Paul was sitting across from me in my office, and I had just finished updating him on my meeting with Charles. I always kind of felt that Paul was jealous of my relationship with Charles, though of course, he had no reason to be. He often gave me grief about Charles's advice, picking it apart and referring to it as "old school." Which is what was happening right now.

"Sounds like something Charles learned about in a conference in the 80s or something. What does that even mean, an undeniable culture?"

"You know, it's...undeniable. A culture so strong and authentic and built into our business that it takes on a life of its own," I said. "I'm not sure we've ever had a culture that strong, but we've certainly come close. I mean, think about the early days of the business, when everyone was pumped to be here and the energy was palpable. I'm not sure how we'll do it, or what exactly we need to do, but at this point it's the best idea we have."

He looked at me skeptically and said, "And that's going to solve our problems? I don't know, Will. Maybe we should just accept the fact that we're going to be acquired, and instead of fighting it and changing everything up, we prepare for what's to come as part of something new. Maybe you could retire!"

"Retire?! Are you crazy? First of all, I'm barely 30 years old..."

"You're 34. I'd hardly say you're barely…"

"And second of all, we haven't been working so hard building this business to let some greedy company come in and take it all away while we're down. No, we're going to fight this, and I'm convinced that Charles is right. It all starts with our culture. It always has," I said.

Realizing that I had stood up during my rant, I sat back down and said, "The other thing I'm going to do is find out who the bastards are that are trying to buy us."

"You're still on that? Seems like a waste of time to me," Paul said. "Who are you going to talk with first?"

"Codeword 9 is first up. Maggs, their CEO, agreed right away to meet, which makes me think he might be the one. You ever meet him?" I asked.

"Nope. Heard him talk once. Seems like a good guy, I guess. And what are you going to do, come right out and ask him?"

I had been thinking about the best approach and decided against being direct.

"No. I'm not going to let on that I'm aware of the process. I don't want to tip my hand that I'm even aware of the acquisition offer, much less trying to subvert it. I'll explain the meeting as part of a bigger relationship-building exercise I'm working on, and see if I can sniff it out of him."

"Sounds like a plan. When's your meeting?"

"This afternoon at…," I said, looking at the calendar on my phone, "3. They're not too far from here. I might walk if the weather stays nice."

Paul and I chatted for a few more minutes before he left for a meeting. I walked over to the corner of my office where the windows came together, giving me an almost 180-degree view of our city. It was a truly beautiful town, and like most cities, we had a park—in our case, Foothills Park—smack in the middle of everything.

From my vantage point, I saw two women running on the west end of the park. They looked like they had been running for a decent amount of time and as they approached the entrance to the park, I saw them stop and chat for a moment. Were they arguing? I couldn't quite tell, but the conversation did seem to be getting heated.

A truck pulled up to the light in front of the park and blocked my view of the runners. I glanced down at my phone and scanned through some emails, and I looked back down just as the truck was pulling away. Now only one of the runners was standing there. Where had the other woman gone? I scanned the area but didn't see her anywhere.

The remaining runner made her way over to a bench and did some stretching exercises for a few minutes. Then she got back on the trail and began running, and I could tell she was moving a decent amount faster than she was earlier.

"Boss?"

I turned and saw Tina poking her head in my office.

“Hey, what’s up?” I asked.

“I just got a message from Maggs’s assistant. He wants to know if you can move the meeting up a bit and meet at 2:30. I know you wanted to walk, and I think if you leave now you can make it. Should I tell him you’ll be there?”

“Yep, tell him I’m on the way,” I said. I looked back down at the park and could no longer see the runner. I guess I needed to get moving as well.

CHAPTER 8

Years ago a major real estate developer in our town had acquired a gigantic office building in a developing area of the city. The building was previously a manufacturing plant and had essentially been vacant for 10 years. His team spent two years and an impressive amount of capital redeveloping the building, essentially re-envisioning it from the ground up.

The ground floor was made up of high-end, locally owned retail establishments. Floors two through four were set up for company offices, some areas cut up into coworking spaces and others large enough for teams with over 100 employees to work in. And floors five through six were condos, allowing people to literally live, work, and play in this one building.

It was a smashing success from the start and one of my favorite spots to meet people for coffee or lunch.

The Codeword 9 office was on the third floor, and as I approached the elevator bank I saw Maggs already standing there, vigorously thumbing away at his phone. I was pretty sure that Maggs was his last name, but since I had never heard him called anything else I couldn't be positive. He was about my height and I was surprised at how casually he was dressed. Of course, I was dressed equally casually, though on this occasion I decided to pair my jeans with my favorite REM shirt rather than our company shirt. No sense heading into enemy territory with a target on my back.

Arriving right as Maggs entered the elevator, I followed him in and asked, "Got room for one more in here?"

"Sure, what floor?" Maggs said before looking up, but then recognizing it was me, said, "Will, great timing! And it's so good to finally meet!"

We shook hands and he pressed the button for the third floor. As the doors closed, I said, "Great to meet you as well. I was so jealous when you guys moved in here. How long ago was that?"

"We were one of the first tenants in the building, actually. So, probably a little over a year I'd guess. But I don't know what you're jealous about, I've heard your office is killer!"

"The views are terrific," I said. "But it seems like the energy in this building must be great for your culture."

The elevator door opened and I followed Maggs out. He led us down the hallway to the right, passing several open coworking areas filled with people hammering away at their laptops. Nondescript pop music was playing lightly in the background, but everyone had headphones on, singularly going about their work in the midst of a crowd. I always loved knocking work out in the middle of a bunch of people…maybe that's why I so frequently left the brilliant views of my personal office in favor of crowded coffee shops when I needed to get real work done.

"The energy here *is* great, no doubt about that," he said. "Our office is just around this corner."

Making the turn, we found ourselves in front of two large glass doors and behind them, in the lobby of their office, a massive Codeword 9 neon sign. Maggs swiped his security badge, the doors made a clicking sound, and he opened the door for me to enter.

Like most advertising agencies, there was frenetic energy about the place. A woman passed us in quite a hurry, giving Maggs a head nod as she dodged us. Three people were engaged in a lively conversation in the hallway, and without stopping their conversation, separated slightly so we could pass.

Maggs led us through the initial entryway and into a large, open area.

"This is the main hub of the agency. It's great because we can use it to have town hall meetings, big group brainstorms, holiday parties, and we even hold networking events for the community here. You should come to one someday, they're a blast," he said.

"I'll have to do that. A bunch of my team members have been to your events and they describe them as more of a party than anything else, which I guess makes them such great networking events."

Maggs smiled and said, "You know our industry, 'work hard, play hard.' Am I right?"

Before I could answer, a man came up to him and whispered something in his ear. Maggs turned to me and said, "Sorry about this, Will, but I need to deal with something. Grab a seat anywhere and I'll be back in five. The Wi-Fi password is on pretty much any whiteboard if you need it."

He bolted off and I looked for a place to sit. I found a comfy-looking sofa that was unoccupied and plopped down in it. Directly across from me was another couch, only that one was much more modern, all leather and sharp edges. The couch I was on was more like one you might find in a living room. In fact, I think we had a similar one in our living room at home.

As I looked around the office, the dichotomy between the two couches seemed to fit the aesthetics of the entire office. There were mismatched cubicles in some areas and all sorts of different types of chairs that people were using. It definitely felt like a company that, as it grew, brought all of the old furniture and office equipment along with it.

Maggs reappeared and said, "Sorry about that. We're working on a big presentation and I needed to make a few decisions. You know how that goes. Why don't we go hang out in one of our conference rooms?"

I followed him through the office, passing one wall that was graffitied by a local artist, another wall with famous advertising campaigns (the "Real Beauty" Dove campaign and the Budweiser "Wassup" campaign among them), and a hallway with old science fiction posters.

The conference room we entered was pretty standard and had a view of the parking lot and surrounding buildings. I grabbed a seat and Maggs opened up a mini-fridge and handed me a bottle of water.

"Thanks," I said. "And thanks for agreeing to meet up. I've been a fan of your agency for a while and realized we never had a chance to meet."

"Yeah, I have to admit," he said, "I was surprised to receive your call. I know we've only really competed a few times, but it's not often your competition calls up and wants to meet."

"True. I guess my feeling is, it's a big world and there are plenty of clients out there, and maybe we could learn a few things from each other that would help our businesses," I said.

Just then, someone knocked on the door. Maggs turned and waved the person in. It was a young woman with probably the brightest shade of red I'd ever seen in someone's hair. She handed Maggs a piece of paper, he quickly looked it over and said, "This looks great," and she exited.

"Sorry, lots going on," he said. "I love the idea. Why don't you get us started and tell me about what's going on in your world."

I jumped in, careful not to let him know that I was aware of the acquisition process, or that we were struggling in any way. I talked about how Paul and I had started the business, our growth over the years, and some projects we were currently working on. He asked a few questions—nothing that led me to believe he was the potential acquirer—and then started telling me about his business.

"...and so now we're a little over 200 people and climbing, and it's a bit tough to keep up with the pace. It feels like everything is moving in 100 different directions."

There was another knock. He looked at me and said, "case in point," as he opened the door. This time, a middle-aged man, dressed sharply (definitely someone in Client Services) entered. Maggs introduced me and then asked what he needed.

"Did you tell Larry about a half-hour ago that we were going with the aggressive approach for the pitch on Friday?" he asked.

"Yes, Larry made some great points and I think it's probably the best approach. Why, you don't?"

"Maggs, this is the third time you've switched the direction on this presentation. Just yesterday you told us all that the best approach was to go with the…," he stopped, looking at me for a second, "…initial strategy. I'm not even sure we have time to change everything to be ready to go aggressive on Friday," he said.

I knew they were using code words, talking in a way so I wouldn't hear anything I shouldn't, but I got the gist. They had a few approaches to a big client pitch, and Maggs was changing direction at the last minute.

"Okay, okay, I hear you," he said. "Let's stick with the initial strategy. Tell Larry I think that's best."

"Great, thanks," he said. "And please, if anyone else tries to change your mind, text me and I'll come running."

He left and the door to the conference room clanged shut. Maggs gave me a we'll see how that goes look, and sat back down.

"So, where were we?" he asked.

"You were talking about how, with the growth, it's tough to keep up with the pace of change," I said.

"Right. That conversation I just had was a great example. I have people coming to me from a million different directions and I honestly can't keep up with it all, so I make mistakes or change my mind. It's like I don't know what my North Star is, nor does my team. Know what I mean?"

This sounded more like someone that needed a therapy session rather than someone who was trying to buy my company. But, I had to dig a little more to be sure.

"I can understand that," I said. "I'm curious if you have an 'end game' for the business. Like, is your goal to grow to a certain point and sell? Or acquire other agencies to build a larger business?"

"Acquire other agencies? Ha, I couldn't imagine trying to layer in another shop on top of this chaos. And maybe at some point I'd like to sell, but I'd have to fix our problems before anyone would be interested, starting with our turnover issues."

"Wait, *you're* having turnover issues? But you're growing so fast!" I said.

"I know, it's shocking to me as well. Consider this: last quarter we hired 18 people, but only nine of those were for new jobs. The other nine were for replacement hires. I can't keep up with how often people are resigning."

He was sharing a great deal with me, so I decided to do the same. I caught him up on our problems—but was careful not to share the acquisition process we were in. After explaining the results of our exit interviews (the reason people said they left our company), I asked if he had done the same.

"Oh yeah, and I expected to hear things about people being upset that they weren't paid enough, or that they weren't promoted fast enough, but the number one reason people gave for leaving our business was that they weren't sure why they were working here. Like, they needed something more than a great salary and benefits. Which I don't get, our parents worked at the same jobs for…"

Before he could finish his rant, which I was sure was going to eventually lead to how young people today just weren't loyal enough, someone else knocked at the door. Again, he apologized, and after talking with the person for a few minutes, he said, "Will, I'm sorry but I'm going to have to cut our meeting short. There's another fire I need to put out. But I'm glad we did this, and let's make it a more regular thing in the future. I assume you know your way out?"

"Yep, no worries, I can show myself out. Thanks for taking the time, Maggs," I said, and he was gone.

On the walk back to my office, I reflected on what I had just experienced. Here was this agency that everyone thought was on top of the world. Crushing it in every way—growth, awards, killer clients…and yet, they were hemorrhaging team members. It sounded like their turnover was worse than ours.

While the mission was to see if Codeword 9 was our potential acquirer—and unless Maggs was an Oscar-level actor I couldn't see that being the case—it was possible that I gained even more from the conversation. Could part of what he was struggling with be a piece of the puzzle I needed to help right our ship?

MONTH 2

CHAPTER 9

Two weeks had passed since my meeting with Maggs, and I was no closer to solving our culture issues, or uncovering which company was attempting to acquire us. Later this week I would meet with the CEO of Massive, and I was betting it was them.

Today I was meeting with Charles. Surprisingly, he wanted to meet at our office, rather than outside doing something physical.

My phone buzzed and I picked it up off my desk. It was a text from Paul:

earth to young skywalker, your yoda has entered the building

I laughed, stuck the phone in my pocket, closed my laptop, and headed toward the lobby.

"...it really was a great trip. I'm surprised you haven't been before," I heard Paul saying to Charles as I rounded the corner.

"Hey Charles, sorry to keep you waiting. Especially with this guy," I said, softly elbowing Paul in the ribs.

Charles and I shook hands, and he said, "Not at all. Paul was just telling me about his recent trip snorkeling with the family. As much as I like adventures, in most cases I try to keep my feet on the ground."

"Okay, I'll leave you guys to it," Paul said. "Great to see you, Charles."

Even though Paul gave me a hard time about Charles, I always thought, deep down, that Paul actually liked him. I began to lead Charles toward my office when he asked if I would take him the long way there.

"I'd like to see more of the vibe, as you called it when we last spoke," he said. So I took a winding way through the space, stopping to introduce him to a few people along the way.

After we made it to my office, two coffees in hand that we picked up from the kitchen area, I closed the door and we both sat down.

"So, what did you think?" I asked.

"About the office? Well," he said, "it definitely feels different from the last time I was here. I'm starting to see what you're talking about. There's a lack of consistent energy throughout the place. I remember the feeling I had the last time you walked me through. I felt inspired, quite honestly."

"And you're feeling a little less so now, I assume?"

"To put it lightly, yes. It's not that people were rude or sleeping on the job, but you can tell when a culture is humming, and I didn't get that feeling from your shop today," he said.

"Is that why you wanted to meet here today?" I asked.

"Partly. After you gave me an overview of your conversation with

Maggs, I thought we might need a whiteboard for our chat today. So, take me through your meeting with him in more detail."

I had given Charles a brief overview of my meeting with Maggs on a call last week, so I spent the next 20 minutes giving him a deeper dive. When I stopped, he got up and walked over to the window, motioning me to join him.

"Did you know that I was on the planning committee for Foothills Park, back when they were initially working on the concept?" he asked, motioning out the window toward the park below.

"Wow, no, I didn't know that. How long ago was that?"

"Oh, well let's see," he said, scratching his chin, "it was almost 20 years ago. Wow, amazing how time flies. In fact, our committee is supposed to be getting back together for a 20-year reunion later this year.

"I'm not sure if you've ever thought about it, but from this vantage point you can see pretty clearly how well-architected the park is. It's a fairly large park, about a quarter the size of Central Park in New York. Look out there and tell me what you see," he said.

I looked down at the park I had traversed so many times—many of them with Charles—and tried to imagine what he was getting at.

"I see lots of people scattered throughout the park. Some are walking or riding the path. There's a group of young men throwing a frisbee in the middle of that field. I see the skatepark and a lot of activity over there…"

"Which area of the park would you describe as 'active'?" he asked.

"Over on that end," I said, pointing to where the playground and skatepark were. "There's a ton of activity over there. Lots of kids playing and parents hanging out together."

"And which part of the park would you describe as 'peaceful'?"

I scanned the park. "The area near the gardens for sure. There are fewer people, and those that I see are mostly reading a book or walking on their own."

I looked back and forth from those two areas and said, "Gosh, I never realized how different those two places in the park are. If you only visited one, you'd think the park was for an entirely different use case."

"Exactly!" Charles said. "A well-designed park is one that makes sure everyone has a place to enjoy. If we had put the playground on one end and the skatepark on another, you'd have a very tough place for a person who wanted some peace and quiet to enjoy. One of the goals is to design a park so that it is enjoyable for the entire community.

"Another thing you probably didn't realize is that a park needs to be, and maybe more importantly feel, safe," he said.

"How do you do that?" I asked.

"There are many ways, all of which include intentional design at the forefront. For instance, when we first put our designs together, we created one main area to enter and leave the park. Our thinking was that it would be terrific to have people essentially forced to interact as they went in and out of the park. Turns out, that's a terrible idea. First of all, not everyone wants to socialize when visiting a park, but more importantly, people need to know that there are many ways in and out. Subconsciously, that will give someone the perception of safety.

"Additionally, you'll notice that there are no dead ends in the park. That is also by design. And lots of open spaces. No vegetation is too high not to be seen around. Visibility is key for a feeling of safety," he said.

"Wow, I've never thought about that. And now that you describe it, I see lighting throughout the park that makes sense based on that strategy," I said.

"Right," Charles responded, "the lighting is very important. So are the placement of benches. I could go on and on, but the point is, planning something like a park takes a long-term vision."

"The group you worked with to plan this must have been experienced at this kind of thing. It's amazing what a great team can do together, isn't it," I said.

Charles laughed out loud at this. "Yes it is, but that is not at all how we started. When I began working with the planning committee, it was an absolute circus. Everyone had different ideas of what features they wanted to be included. We spent months going in circles about what this park could and should be, and when we finally had a semblance of a plan together, it looked a lot like Frankenstein's monster, with random components bolted on with seemingly no continuity."

"How did you get from that point to where it is today?" I asked.

"Well, we had a plan, which by the way, we thought was terrific. Remember, we were Dr. Frankenstein in this example, so we believed what we had was an amazing design. We took the plan to a leading architect in town to get his advice. He was a pretty cut-to-the-chase, raw kinda guy, and if I remember correctly his first question to us was, 'So which of your kids drew this up?' After the initial shock wore off we settled in to listen to his feedback. And what I learned from him changed the course of my life forever."

"What did he teach you?" I asked.

"That," he said, "is why I need a whiteboard. And a second coffee wouldn't hurt."

I grabbed my notepad and we made our way to the nearest conference room, picking up another coffee for Charles on the way.

He grabbed a marker and walked to the whiteboard. Turning to me, he said, "What do you think the major issue is with Codeword 9, based on what Maggs shared?"

"Well," I said, "it seems pretty clear that they aren't very focused, and Maggs, as good a guy as he seems, doesn't really know how to lead them forward."

"And," Charles said, "more importantly, Maggs himself doesn't know where the company is going. The company has no foundation. Or, what I like to call, an 'Authentic Foundation.'"

He wrote at the top of the whiteboard:

Authentic Foundation

"It seems to me, without an Authentic Foundation, you can't build an Undeniable Culture, which is what you're after, correct?" he asked.

"Absolutely," I said.

"Great. So the first thing that the architect told us was that we clearly had no real direction for our project. He started asking us a lot of 'why' questions. Why is this park needed? Why should it exist? Why should people care?

"And we clearly had no good answers to those questions, or at least no consistent answers that we all believed in. He then sent us away and told us to come back when we had those answers," he said.

"How long did that take?" I asked.

"Way too long, but we eventually got to a place we felt good about. So we set up another meeting with the architect and shared what we came up with," he said.

"And what was it? Do you remember?" I asked.

He rubbed his chin for a minute and said, "I think it was something like: to create a healthy, connected, inclusive, supportive community. Something like that. He pressure-tested it with us, mostly by asking more 'why' questions, and ultimately he agreed that we had landed on something solid. He then informed us that was our Purpose. It was our 'why,'" he said.

He wrote the word *Purpose* on the whiteboard.

"Then he asked us what we envisioned the park to be in three to five years. Not 10 years, not 20 years, but three to five years. He said it was important to be able to 'see' where you want to take the project, and in his experience, if you push that more than five years you risk the chance of losing your way. So he sent us off again and we worked on that question.

"A few months later we came back and shared our plan, and he informed us that we now had our Vision. He explained that the goal was for the Purpose to be evergreen—that ideally it would never change—but our Vision is something we should reassess every year. Vision can change, but Purpose rarely does," he said.

"I love that. So with the Purpose and Vision, your team now had a foundation, or I suppose you'd call that an 'Authentic Foundation,' to go forward with," I said.

"Exactly. And after I learned the importance of Purpose and Vision from the architect, I spent years working that into my businesses and eventually realized there were two components missing. One might be obvious to you by now, and that's Values. You can have a Purpose that explains why you're doing what you're doing, and you can have a Vision that shows where you're headed, but Values are needed in order to tell you how to behave along the journey," he said.

He wrote on the whiteboard:

Authentic Foundation

Step #1: PVTV

Purpose

Vision

Values

"Does that make sense?" he asked.

"I think so, sure. It's one thing to know why you're on the journey, another to know where you're headed, and yet another to know how you'll behave. It seems like one thing is missing though, and I'm guessing that's why you left the blank between Vision and Values," I said.

"And what might that be?" he asked.

"To me what's missing is the 'how.'"

"Bingo. I call that your Tenets. They're the things you need to do in order to achieve your Vision," he said, updating the whiteboard.

Purpose - ***why you exist***

Vision - ***where you're headed (3-5 years)***

Tenets - ***how you will accomplish your Vision***

Values - ***how you will behave***

"Will, I've been waiting to share this PVTV construct with you for the right time, and I think this is it. I've used PVTV to help my companies and other businesses over the years find their true center, and from that build incredible businesses and, as we discussed, undeniable cultures. I think it's required if you want to strengthen your business and get back on track," he said.

I sat back and looked at the whiteboard, absorbing what he had just told me. We had exactly none of those things established at my company. Sure, we talked about Values but we weren't living them and I doubt anyone could even name one. I could maybe name two.

We spent the next 20 minutes with Charles giving me examples of how to bring our PVTV to life once we had developed it. According to him, the execution of your Purpose is far more important than actually having it. In fact, a well-developed and thoughtful Purpose that you don't use is more of a negative than not having one at all.

"How is that the case? I would have thought just having a Purpose defined is at least a positive step," I said.

"Let's assume you develop your Purpose statement with your entire company, which is highly recommended. First, with your leadership team, and then with everyone. If you do it right, everyone will be excited, if not a little skeptical. Purpose always brings out the skeptics, justifiably so, because so few leaders and companies actually believe in their Purpose and execute on it. If you then do nothing with it from that point forward, the team will believe less in you than they did before, and, sadly they will believe less in the power of Purpose," he explained.

I thought about that for a moment. "I get that. So, I need to develop, along with the team, our PVTV and then formulate a plan to bring it to life. What's next?"

"Your assignment, if you choose to accept it," he said, giving me a smile, "is to come up with a list of things that you think are required to build an Authentic Foundation for a business. Obviously, PVTV will be at the start, and heart, of that list," he said.

"You're giving me a homework assignment? Just kidding, I love it, and I'll have a list for you the next time we meet," I said.

I asked him a few questions about the best way to come up with our PVTV. His advice was for me to work with the leadership team to create an initial draft, then work with the entire firm to crystallize it.

After he left, I asked Tina if she could look at the schedules for the leadership team and book us a two-hour meeting next week. When she asked me what to call the meeting, I thought for a moment and said, "Call it: Day One."

For more depth on Purpose, Vision, Tenets & Values (PVTV), read *The 5-Day Turnaround* and *The Great Team Turnaround*. *The Great Team Turnaround* specifically goes into the ways to bring PVTV to life and how to measure its effects.

CHAPTER 10

I arrived 20 minutes early at the coffee shop for my meeting with Mark, the CMO of RedBrick, and grabbed a booth toward the back. I typically preferred to sit at one of the tables in the middle of the cafe, but today I would need some privacy for our conversation.

The Steaming Cup had been my favorite place for meetings since it opened a few years back. The coffee was always hot, the staff was friendly (and knew me by name at this point, which was fun), and it was a short walk from the office.

It had always been my habit to arrive early to meetings like this, both to make sure I wasn't late (ever!) but also to allow myself to prepare mentally. I always found that if I'm running late, I arrive scattered and apologetic, making it hard to get the most out of the meeting.

My goal with Mark today was to find out what I could about the RFP process for their account, what they liked about Massive (our competition for the business), and if possible, what we needed to do to win. Mark and I had a solid relationship and I knew he'd shoot me straight.

I also assumed that if I wanted any chance of stopping the sale of my company, I'd need to secure a big win like this in order to change the minds of my board members. A loss of the RedBrick account right before they made their final decision would be too much to overcome.

So, yes, one could say a lot was riding on this one.

Mark entered the cafe right on time. He wore a dark gray suit with a black checkered tie, and he was easy to pick out because he was the only person in the cafe wearing a suit. I'd actually never seen Mark in anything but a suit—and he probably never saw me in anything other than jeans and a company shirt.

I waved him over and he made his way over to me.

"Hey Will, how was your weekend?" he asked as he slid into the booth.

"Great, how about yours? Getting any sleep with that new baby?" I asked.

"Well, as I know you're well aware, sleep is not something many parents can brag about. But honestly, our daughter started sleeping through the night at about six weeks old and has been a consistent sleeper ever since. I better knock on wood for that," he said, clicking his knuckles on the cherry walnut table.

"Oh man, I'm so jealous, our daughter didn't sleep well for almost her first year, and even now it's 50/50 whether or not she ends up in our bed," I said.

He laughed and grabbed a menu, thumbing through the coffee selections. A waiter came over and Mark ordered a soy latte.

We caught up a little more on each other's lives until Mark's coffee came. Then I said, "Thanks for meeting up today. Steve told me about the RFP process you guys are running, and we're excited to be a part of it."

"And we're happy to have you guys as a part of it. We had several agencies on our roster, and I just decided that it would be better to consolidate all of that work into one partner to make things easier for our team, and hopefully make the work more consistent," he said.

This was a typical process in the marketing agency world. Brands such as RedBrick go through cycles of preferring to have specialty shops work on various aspects of their business—one shop for advertising, one for website development, one for email marketing, etc.—and then ultimately decide that's too inefficient, opting for one agency that could do all the work.

"I appreciate the vote of confidence to make it to the final two. And Steve said the shop we're up against is Massive, is that right?" I asked.

"Yep, you and Massive. The RFP should be sent to you all in a month or two," he said.

"Great, I've heard good things about Massive but I like our chances," I said, smiling.

"Have you met Wes before?" he asked. Wes was the CEO of Massive.

"No, but funny enough, we're meeting next week. I decided to get to know my competition a little, and he was gracious enough to accept. Well, I wouldn't say gracious, but he did accept," I said.

Mark smiled and said, "That does sound like Wes. He's a good guy, but he's very intense, kind of a no-nonsense type of leader. He does run a tight shop and his team is always on point. I'll be curious to hear what you think of him after the meeting."

"I'm looking forward to it. I do have a question for you. I know the RFP will list out in detail what you're looking for, but I'm curious what *you* are looking for in a partner."

I learned early on to pose this question to the ultimate decision-maker. While the organization would list out very specific items in a formal RFP, if you asked the person making the call what was most important to them, they'd often share an insight that wasn't listed.

"That's a great question, Will," he said. He took a minute to continue, obviously thinking about his answer. "Both of your agencies have great team members and have done good work for us, but what I'm looking for is an agency that really stands for something."

"Could you tell me more about what you mean by that?" I asked.

"Sure, might as well be fully honest with you," he said. "Ever hear of The Chopping Blade agency?"

Laughing, I said, "No, but where do we come up with these names?"

"I know. Some of them sound like they should be the name of a rock band. So basically, and here comes the honest part, if I had the budget that I asked for from my CEO, I'd hire The Chopping Blade to be our agency. No RFP process needed."

Wow. I wasn't expecting that. To know that even if we won we'd be second fiddle in Mark's mind was not a great feeling.

"I appreciate your honesty, but I have to ask, what is it about them that makes them the clear favorite in your mind?"

Mark then spent the next five minutes talking about how great The Chopping Blade was. He saw the CEO speak at an event, they ran that award-winning campaign, he knows this CMO that loves them...it was a bit nauseating.

Eventually, he said, "I guess the real reason I'm such a fan is that, in my mind, they stand for creativity, pure and simple. Everything they talk about, everything they do, screams: *'We produce great creative, and creative is everything to us.'*

"What I really want to see from you and Massive is what either of you stands for. What makes you great? What does your entire team rally around?" he said.

I realized at that moment that I didn't have an answer. There was not one single thing that I could point to that I could honestly say was what we stood for. Yes, we also thought creativity was important, but we also thought technology was important, as were our client relationships. If you asked our sales team what the most important thing to us was, they'd say growth.

"That, uh," I said, stammering a bit, "is really interesting, Mark. Thanks for sharing that, and it makes total sense. I don't want to spoil the surprise about what our one thing is, but rest assured it will come through loud and clear in our response to the RFP."

He smiled in a way that said, *I'll pretend you're not bluffing.* "Sounds good. I really look forward to it and thanks for letting me be honest. And who knows, maybe down the road I'll be saying the same thing about your shop—minus the 'we can't afford you' part, I hope."

We both laughed, and after a few more minutes of conversation, he exited, leaving me in the booth to think about what I had just heard.

What *do* we stand for?

I pulled out my notebook and opened it to the notes I had taken in my meeting with Charles. On a fresh page, I began working on Charles's homework assignment. I wrote:

Authentic Foundation

1. Purpose, Vision, Tenets, and Values (PVTV)

2. Core Identity

I'd have to vet this with Charles, but it felt right. You must know why your company exists, where you're headed, how you're going to get there, and how you'll behave along the way. Charles's PVTV format would address that. But you also needed to know what you stood for as a company, which I called: Core Identity. I could see those two elements as critical to creating an Authentic Foundation, which ultimately would help unlock an Undeniable Culture.

I was sure there was something else I was missing, but I was interrupted by an alert from my phone. Time to head back to work for a meeting.

CHAPTER 11

We decided to hold the company offsite at Intown Video Games, a retro event and gaming business that was about a 15-minute drive from our office. We'd meet from 10 a.m. until 4 p.m., with the last two hours allotted for video games and social time. I always thought it was best to incorporate some fun at offsite events.

I arrived 45 minutes early along with the rest of the Leadership Team (minus Paul, who showed up about 10 minutes later than everyone else in a kind of silent protest). The room we'd be using was a gigantic, open space with tables and whiteboards throughout. It was the perfect setting to inspire the kind of thinking we'd need today.

Getting to this day was a bit...laborious. What I thought would be an easy process, landing on a rough draft of our Purpose, Vision, Tenets, and Values, was decidedly not. As usual, it started with Paul.

As soon as I got back to the office after my meeting with Mark, I pulled Paul into my office to share what I had learned from both Charles and Mark.

"Will, no offense, but it really seems like you're grasping at straws here. Now, four months out from a likely sale of the company, with our biggest new business pitch ever on the horizon, you want us to create some new kind of operating model? Don't we have bigger things to work on?" Paul said.

"And I don't even know what Mark was talking about, 'What's

our one thing?' That sounds almost just as silly as Charles's PPTV or whatever," he added.

"It's PVTV—Purpose, Vision, Tenets, and Values," I said, knowing he was butchering it on purpose. "And on the contrary, I think now is the absolute best time to be working on these things. If we want to have any chance to save our company—and win the pitch with RedBrick— we have to shake things up and get this team motivated!"

I realized I was getting animated and was probably close to shouting, so I took a deep breath and sat down on the couch. "Listen," I said, "I know you're not fully on board with trying to stop this acquisition process, but even if we do get acquired, you must agree that having our team performing at our best is going to help everything go more smoothly. I really believe that this kind of work *on* our business, instead of just *in* our business, is what we need right now."

While I wasn't always good at doing it, I was a big believer in the importance of leaders prioritizing working on their business rather than only in their business. It is far too easy to get swept up in the momentum of building your team or business and realizing you're in "get it done" mode too often, rarely lifting your head up to see what might need to be course-corrected. That is exactly what had happened to our company and I was sure of it.

"Well, I just feel like I'm here trying to figure out what's going on and how we can strengthen the business, and you're out there getting advice from people on how to change everything that we've been working on for years," he said.

One of the many things I learned from Sarah over the course of our relationship was that sometimes it's better to listen and be supportive rather than trying to solve another person's problems. I had a tendency to either get defensive or try to fix the problem. Sometimes it was better to show that you understood the person's frustration. This felt like one of those times.

"I can see how it might look like that, Paul, and I'm sorry. I don't want you to feel like you're here alone working on this problem. I'm happy to dig in with you and help where I can. And you know Charles is basically a part of this team and has given us advice and counsel over the years. I know I hold him in the highest regard, perhaps a bit more than you do, but I do weigh everything he says before simply acting on it," I said.

Paul gave me a nod that seemed to say both *Thanks for hearing me out* and *I guess I have to get on board with this*, which I took as the best response I was going to get.

The meeting later that day with the Leadership Team, which I had called, "Day One," was a bit easier, though the hard work of fleshing out an initial rough draft of our PVTV took some time. Overall, the team liked the idea of creating a foundation like PVTV, and in fact, most seemed to be craving it once we dove in.

By the end of the session, we had a strong Vision Statement ("To be sought-after by the world's best companies for our creative problem-solving") and solid Tenets to go along with it, but the Purpose and Values still needed a lot of work. The essence was there, but they needed more depth.

"I was really hoping we'd have this in a pretty tight place before the offsite. Maybe we should fit in one more meeting on this?" I asked.

"Actually," said Rachel, "I think we're in a great spot! I would imagine the elements of your PVTV that you most want everyone weighing in on would be the Purpose and Values."

"I buy that," said Steve. "Plus, if it means we don't have to have another one of these meetings..."

Laughing, I said, "Okay, I agree, but not in order to spare Steve another meeting. Let's roll with this and see how the team comes together around our Purpose and Values."

If you want more detail on building out your PVTV, Will takes a team through the step-by-step process of creating their Purpose, Vision, Tenets, and Values in *The Great Team Turnaround*. (By then he's become somewhat of an expert.)

Team members started arriving around 9:50 a.m. There was assigned seating, with Post-Its on tables throughout the room indicating where each person would sit. We had placed people strategically to get a good cross section of team members working together, trying to pair people who rarely interacted during the workday. A new company T-shirt lay over each chair. I was big on company swag, always looking for an excuse to give our team a new item with our logo on it. We had hats, sweatshirts, tote bags, notepads...you name it, we probably had it. And I knew most of the team would show up today wearing some of those items.

People mingled and caught up, grabbing coffee and pastries in the process. At 10:15, I grabbed the mic at the front of the room and asked everyone to find their seats so we could get started.

"Welcome to our company offsite. I think you'll agree that our theme today, 'Gaming Our Business,' is pretty on the nose," I said. "And don't worry, Kyle, we will have time to play video games at the end of the day."

Kyle was one of our resident gamers. In fact, we had a lot of gamers on the team, mostly in the creative and tech departments.

"This meeting has been a long time coming. We've built a strong business over the years, and you all should be proud, as I am, of what we've created. And today we're going to focus on why we're working so hard to build this business. The Purpose of what we do. We'll leave here today with a foundational blueprint that will guide us for years to come," I said.

Then, using the giant whiteboard behind me, I started explaining the concept of PVTV, walking them through each component—Purpose, Vision, Tenets, and Values—and filling in the areas that our leadership team had already created.

After the explanation, and some questions from the team, I informed them that they would all be paired with a leadership team member to begin brainstorming their way through our PVTV.

As the teams got to work, I began roaming the room, listening in on conversations and weighing in when I thought it would be helpful.

"Okay, where are you guys on our Purpose statement," I asked one of the teams.

"I think our Purpose would be to build great websites," one team member said.

Another team member said, "But we do more than just build websites. We create email campaigns, help our customers with branding, and many other areas of marketing."

"Yeah," the first team member said, "but the majority of our sales come from website builds."

I jumped in. "What you two are talking about is *what* we do. A Purpose is *why* we do it."

"Because you pay us to do it!" the first one said, laughing.

"Sure, but hopefully that's not really why you work so hard and take such pride in the work you do," I said.

"Let's try a quick exercise," I continued, remembering a tip Charles had given me to work through finding a company's Purpose. "Do I have a brave volunteer?"

Everyone in the group kind of looked at one another, and finally one of our creatives, Ashley, raised her hand.

"Great, extra points for Ashley. And you're a great person for this exercise because I know for a fact that you take great pride in your work," I said. "Okay, why do you work hard to produce such great creative? Let's say for a client's new website."

"I guess because I want to deliver a good product to the client?" she said, a little uncertain.

"Why?"

"Because I want whoever is going to use that website to have a good experience."

"Why?"

She thought for a moment. "I guess because I want the person who experiences what I created to be…satisfied."

"Okay, great! Why don't you guys see if that concept holds up. Maybe what we create as an agency is ultimately to make people's lives better."

The team began pressure-testing that concept as I walked away. I had similar conversations with other teams, all ending up in a similar place. I kind of liked that direction—making people happy through what we did—and it was very different from where the leadership team was ending up at our previous session.

After a few hours, we broke for lunch and I asked each team to share where they ended up with our Purpose statement. It became pretty clear that the central theme was making people happy, both through the work that we produced and the interactions we had with our clients.

When lunch was over, I sent the teams back to work, but this time on our Values. I emphasized that our Values should be representative of how we want to behave on our journey, and should be expressed as, "We believe in..."

While the teams got to work, I pulled two of our best writers out and began working with them on polishing our Purpose based on everyone's feedback.

At 2, after checking in on each team and feeling good about their progress, I let them escape to begin playing video games. I kept the two writers with me (giving them coupons for a free day at the arcade since they were missing it), and they joined me and the leadership team as we began working on pulling the entire PVTV together.

We very quickly got to a solid place and most of the hard work came in nitpicking about each word. By 3:45 we were done, giving us a few minutes before everyone came back together.

I wrote the new PVTV on the big whiteboard in the front of the room and then covered it up with giant Post-Its we brought with us to the event. I then went through the arcade telling everyone to be back in the event space by 4 so we could wrap up.

After everyone was seated, I let them share stories of their video game playing, quickly learning who among them was the most competitive. Steve shared with everyone that he was a competitive Donkey Kong player when he was a teenager, prompting someone from the back to yell, "What's Donkey Kong?" This got a big laugh from everyone, though I wasn't sure if the person was joking.

"Okay, I'm glad everyone had a good time. And I have no idea what Steve was talking about from the olden days. What did you call it, Donkey King?" I said, to more laughter.

"But the real reason we came together today was to create our PVTV. I'm so excited about where we ended up, and so without further ado..."

I pulled down the post-its to expose the PVTV on the whiteboard. It read:

> ***Our Purpose is to Inspire Happiness through positive relationships, impactful work, and doing good.***
>
> ***Our Vision is to be sought-after by the world's best companies for our creative problem-solving.***
>
> ***(Our Tenets) We will do this by attracting and retaining exceptional people, building remarkable products and experiences, and striving for operational excellence.***
>
> ***(Our Values) We believe in putting the team first, thinking positively, celebrating diversity, doing good, and having fun.***

After giving everyone time to read it, I asked if anyone had any thoughts.

One of the designers in the back said, "I love the idea of inspiring happiness. I think it can go in many different directions, including how we treat each other. It just feels like...us!"

Another team member, this time from the Client Services team, said, "Is this something that we will use internally only, or is it for external use too? Like, can we show this to clients?"

"That's a great question," I said. "The most important thing is that we live into our PVTV internally. It has to be real to us and we have to live it daily. Beyond that, I think we can decide as we go along how public we want to make it."

Someone asked what we meant by "creative problem-solving." I let the group discuss that amongst themselves, ultimately agreeing that we wanted to be known for helping our clients solve their problems and achieve their goals, and it was a great catch-all for the wide variety of services we offer.

After a few more back and forth discussions—the team was really getting excited about it—I noticed that we were out of time.

"Okay, everyone, we did great work today," I said. "I can see that you're all on board with our PVTV, and I agree with what Susan said earlier. 'Inspiring happiness' really feels like us. As important as it is that we have a defined Purpose, Vision, Tenets, and Values, it's ultimately worthless if we don't put it into action on a daily basis. I want everyone to be thinking of ways to bring our PVTV to life every day. And find ways to recognize your teammates as they exhibit aspects of our PVTV, especially our Values."

"Oh, and one more thing," I added. "We talked to the owner and he's willing to let us stay an extra hour playing more games, so you'll have a little more time to settle who's really the best at Space Invaders."

After a chorus of "What's Space Invaders?" they went running off to the arcade. I was really happy with where we landed today, but I knew it would take hard work to make sure our PVTV was effective in reshaping our culture.

Bird by bird, I felt like we were making progress. The big question was, would the change we were looking for happen fast enough?

CHAPTER 12

Massive's headquarters was located in the largest building in town (a little too fitting if you ask me).

I scanned the map in the lobby and saw that Massive was on the 31st floor, the Penthouse Suite. I tried to push the button for 31 but it wouldn't highlight.

"You have to get security to buzz you in for that floor," a young woman said as she pushed the button for the 24th floor.

"Really? Makes you wonder what they're doing up there that's so important," I said.

"Whatever it is, I'm sure it's big time," she replied, nodding at their name on the wall.

"Nice one," I said. "Have a great day, and thanks for the advice."

I made my way over to the security desk and, after giving my name and driver's license, the security guard found me on the list and walked me back to the elevators. He used his key card to unlock the elevator and sent me on my way.

The elevator doors opened and I was immediately greeted by a woman who said, "You must be Will. Hi, I'm Jo Ann, it's great to meet you."

She gave me a very firm handshake (maybe a bit too firm) and led me into the lobby. "Please have a seat, Wes will be right with you."

I sat down and looked around at the office. Glass, polished silver, and sharp edges dominated the motif. The lobby was immaculate, everything seeming to be perfectly in its place. Even the books on the coffee table in front of me seemed to be perfectly layered on top of each other. I grabbed one, a recent issue of *Fortune* magazine, and began thumbing through it.

I recognized Wes from the cover of a recent local newspaper article. He looked exactly like he did in that shot—his blonde hair sculpted just so, his blue suit pressed and fitted, as well as his tie, belt, and shoes a perfect match. He must have had a personal tailor.

He saw me sitting on the couch and came over, saying, "Will, I hope you weren't waiting too long. Sometimes Jo Ann has a hard time remembering to tell me that I have a guest waiting."

I took a quick glance at Jo Ann and saw her grimace. I was sure she had messaged Wes as soon as I had arrived.

"No worries at all, I just got here," I said, tossing the magazine on the table and shaking his hand.

I saw him look down at the magazine and give a quick glance at Jo Ann, who seemed to be overly attentive to anything Wes was doing. He said, "How about a quick tour?"

"That would be great—I love checking out creative offices," I said. He led me down a hallway, and as we were exiting the lobby I noticed Jo Ann run over to the coffee table and put the magazine I had dropped in the exact place it was before.

As we made our way through the office, it was hard to see what must have been spectacular views of the city because there were personal offices along all the outside walls.

"The view," I said, peering through one of the offices, "looks pretty great. Kind of hard to see, though, unless you have a personal office."

"It is a great view," he said, proudly, "and I use it as a motivator for the team. Around here, you have to earn that view. The better you perform, the better your chances of getting a personal office."

The inside area of the office, where it appeared most of the team worked, was full of high-walled cubicles. Every person I saw in one of the personal offices was wearing a suit or dress.

"I notice everyone dresses very well here," I said, suddenly a bit self-conscious about what I was wearing.

He looked at me, very obviously looking down at my T-shirt and jeans. "I've always believed that you dress for success, Will. In fact," he said, lowering his voice, "the team doesn't know it but I've never promoted anyone that doesn't consistently dress nicely."

Based on how Jo Ann focused so intently on Wes in the lobby, I was pretty sure the team was well aware of that fact.

High on the wall above all the cubicles was the phrase, "Never Stop The Hustle," written by a graffiti artist. It wasn't like street graffiti, more...corporate, if that's a thing.

We continued to make our way through the office. Wes, with a huge smile on his face, would wave to someone and say, "Hey, Sam, how's it going?" and "What's new, Brenda?" He didn't usually wait for a response, and when the person did respond I could tell he was a bit annoyed by having to stop and engage with them for a minute.

As soon as we were out of sight, his smile would quickly disappear. He seemed like a politician, and not the genuine kind.

At the end of the hall, he led me into a beautiful corner office. It was easily twice the size of any other personal office I had seen.

"This is where I make it happen," he said. "I'm sure you have something similar in your building. You know, we looked at that building a few years back as a possible relocation," he said.

I entered his office and sat down on the leather couch against the window (I couldn't help noticing that this made it hard for a guest in his office to see the view), and said, "You seem to have a great relationship with your team."

He looked a little confused, and then said, "Oh, you mean because I was saying hi to everyone? Funny. Let me tell you a little secret."

He stood back up and closed the door to his office. After sitting back down, he said, "I learned this from my father, who was also a very successful entrepreneur. See, I always have a running list in my head of who is performing well and who isn't. As I walk through the office and say hi to people, I either point at them or wave at them. Pointing at someone means, 'you're safe.' But waving at someone means, 'you're going to be fired soon.' It's like a little running joke I have inside my head. You know how it is, you have to keep a tight leash on these people."

I wasn't sure how to react to that, and I definitely did not "know how it is." And I didn't like the fact that he felt like I would be cool with treating people in such a way.

Deciding to change the subject, I said, "So, I appreciate you taking the time to meet up. Shame we haven't done this sooner. I just felt like we should get to know each other..."

"Oh, I get it," he said, interrupting me. "Sun Tzu, right? *'If you know the enemy and know yourself, you need not fear the result of a hundred battles. If you know yourself but not the enemy, for every victory gained you will also suffer a defeat. If you know neither the enemy nor yourself, you will succumb in every battle.'* Makes perfect sense."

"Wow, you memorized that?"

"I've memorized all of Sun Tzu, of course," he said, as if that was a normal thing to do. "In fact, I'm surprised I didn't think of this sooner. As soon as you reached out, I made it a point to get in touch with a few other leaders in town to get to know them as well. Always gotta stay one step ahead of the competition, right?"

"I...guess," I said. "But really, I just wanted to hear more about your business and see if we could learn things from each other."

"Uh huh," he said skeptically.

Just then there was a knock on his door. "Come in," he said.

A woman in a dark gray dress opened the door and, seeing that Wes had a guest, said, "Oh, sorry, I can come back later."

"I said you could come in, what do you need?" Wes asked.

"I just wanted to let you know that the… 'Special Project'…had an issue…," again with the code words, "and I needed some help making a decision."

Wes got up and they huddled at the doorway to his office. I could see he was getting animated even though he was speaking in hushed tones. At one point I heard him say, "How incompetent can you *be*?"

When they finished, he came back in and, before he shut the door, I noticed that the woman had tears in her eyes.

"Everything okay?" I asked. "She seemed pretty upset."

"Oh, yeah," he said, looking back at the door. "As you know, while running a business, especially a business like advertising, you'll make everyone on your team cry at some point. If you don't, you're not really doing your job as a leader. You have to push people, sometimes past their breaking point, to be their best."

Once again, I was speechless.

Remembering that Rachel had told me that Massive was rumored to have the highest turnover in our industry, I suddenly realized why. I also realized I was not a fan of Wes, and needed to get away from him as quickly as I could. But first, I had to find out if he was the one trying to buy my company.

"Where were we?" he asked.

"You were just about to tell me a little about Massive, and I was..."

"Oh, right," he said, cutting me off, "I'm sure you've heard but we're crushing it. Each of the last three years we've grown by 50%. We're the largest agency in the city, and it's not even close."

"With all that growth, I'm curious what keeps you up at night?" I asked.

"Why is it that everyone always asks me that question? I sleep like a baby! But, if I had to point to one thing that is bothering me, it's my leadership team's inability to do their jobs and stop whining! They keep coming to me with their problems with each other, and it's driving me nuts."

"Do you have trouble with them supporting one another? I've found that if my team isn't in lockstep, the rest of the company doesn't know what direction we're headed in," I said.

He gave me an "Aren't you just the cutest" look and said, "I can see how a smaller shop might work that way, but once you become sizable like us, the goal is to have everyone competing, especially at the highest level. I want my leaders exhibiting that behavior—they need to have a killer instinct and the drive and hustle to climb any mountain."

"And if the rest of the team is hearing conflicting messages?"

"That's part of life! If our team members can't figure out who to follow then they're probably not Massive material. It's a competitive world out there, and I only want winners on my team."

Yikes. That sounded like the most dysfunctional way to run a company I've ever heard. But it did make me wonder if my leadership team was doing some of this, even if unintentionally. Was I giving them clear direction? Had I stressed the importance of backing each other up?

I could see now, with Wes's warped sense of leadership, the dysfunction that he was manifesting within the company, and the resulting employee turnover, that his company was growing only because they were making so many acquisitions.

"I'm curious how the acquisitions your company has made in the past have worked out," I said.

He nodded his head and smiled. "I love acquiring businesses. It's the best way to grow. Get all that revenue in one pop. BANG! And you can cut the fat—typically, 15% of the people can be let go straightaway. Plus, you're killing a competitor!"

He sat back in his seat, obviously pleased with what he had just said. I could imagine him lighting up a cigar and cackling amidst the smoke.

"I get that, but isn't organic growth the most profitable and healthiest for an agen…"

"Organic growth? Are you kidding?" he said, cutting me off again. "When you can buy a company and immediately get several million dollars in revenue AND cut people to save money, that's like having to grow a dozen clients. Organic growth is cute if you want to stay a boutique agency, but the real money is in acquisitions."

This could easily be the guy that was trying to buy my shop. He freaking loved buying companies. And gutting them, which is why I really needed to make sure it wasn't him.

"Are there any 'musts' you have when acquiring? We're thinking of getting into that game as well and I could use some pointers from someone who's been so successful at it," I said, carefully stroking his ego so he'd continue to share.

"I always say there are three things that have to be in place for me to acquire another agency," he said. "First, they have to be a direct competitor. What's the point of taking a shop off the market if it doesn't immediately remove your competition?"

We fit that to a tee. If he acquired my agency, he'd win the RedBrick account by default.

"Second, it has to be large enough to make it worth the effort. No small, 10-person shops. I need girth if I'm going to buy an agency."

Again, could be us…

"And lastly, and this is the most important, the CEO has to be willing to stay on for several years. I learned that the hard way. Even though my instinct is to kick them to the curb, if they don't stay then there's a big risk that the top clients won't stay and an even bigger risk that the employees—the ones I actually want to keep—might leave as well. If you buy a company and immediately clients and team members leave, then you're pretty much screwed. That might be the biggest requirement I have," he said. "Plus, I get to control one of my competitors and see them walking around my office, doing what I say. There's nothing like it."

Whew, that definitely didn't apply to my shop. I was happy when I realized that Codeword 9 wasn't trying to buy us, but I was downright ecstatic and also relieved that it wasn't Wes. Now that I had the info I wanted, I needed to get out of there fast. And maybe take an hour-long shower to wash off the dirtiness I felt from simply being near this guy.

Looking at my watch I said, "Oh, wow, time really does fly when you're…talking to someone. Looks like I have to run. Thanks for the time, it was very…enlightening."

If he was put off by the sudden end of our meeting, he didn't show it. He walked me back through the office to the elevator bank.

"And, Will, if you ever want to be acquired by Massive, let me know. I've heard good things about your shop and I'm sure there are some great things we could do together. I need a new Head of Project Management and I think you'd be perfect. Let me know," he said, and with that, he put me on the elevator and pushed the button for the bottom floor.

CHAPTER 13

Today's board meeting, the first since they dropped the bomb on me, was set for 10:30 a.m. Paul and I were in my office going over the final points on the agenda. He was noticeably calmer than I was, which did help to settle my nerves a bit.

"It's going to be fine," he said. "We have some good things to present today. Our numbers, if not showing much growth, are solid. And we can let them know about being in the final two for the RedBrick account. I'm sure they'll be excited about that."

"But I don't have anything tangible to show them in terms of how we're fixing the company," I said.

"I still don't fully agree that there is anything to 'fix,' Will," he said. "We're a growing startup that has the typical 'growing startup' problems."

"Yes, but those typical problems have resulted in our board being willing to sell the company out from under us. To me, that raises our problems from 'typical' to 'disastrous,'" I said. "And I…I mean, *we*…need to figure out a way to make sweeping changes in time for the board to see the potential that we have as a business!"

There was a knock at the door to my office and Tina poked her head in. "Hey guys, some board members are starting to arrive. I have coffee set up, and lunch will be here around 11:45."

"Great, thanks," I said.

Paul and I grabbed our stuff and as we exited my office, he said, "Don't worry, it'll be a good meeting. We're ready."

15 minutes later I once again found myself at the head of the conference room with my board—and this time, Paul—in attendance. We had made it through the awkward part of seeing each other once again after the last meeting, and it was time to get rolling.

"It's great to see all of you again," I said. "Paul and I have been hard at work since our last meeting, and we have a lot of great updates to share."

I clicked forward on the PowerPoint presentation and walked them through the agenda.

"But before I start, I want to make sure you all understand that we're working extremely hard to prove to you that now would be the absolute worst time to sell the business. We've made some great progress along that front, but we won't be sharing any of that today. As you saw from the agenda, our meeting today will be very similar to past meetings.

"I do want to ask though, to just get it out of the way, if there are any updates from your side on the acquisition process," I said. Paul looked down and scratched his head, obviously annoyed that I asked the question. How could I not?

I looked around the room and once again all the board members were avoiding eye contact with me. Most were looking to James to speak up.

"Sure, we can give you a quick update," James said, clearing his throat. "The acquiring company is still very much interested. We've shared the baseline financials that you provided us, and they're putting together a deeper list of due diligence for us to share with them."

"There is one other thing," Linda said. James gave her a terse look, but she continued anyway. "What? I'm tired of this cloak-and-dagger stuff. Listen, Will, apparently they're aware that you are trying to shake things up with the company and they've suggested that by doing that, you might drop the value of the business. They want you to run the business as usual."

I could feel my heart start to beat a little faster. How could they know what I was doing inside the company? The board wasn't even aware. Were they somehow spying on us?

"Will," Paul said, bringing me back to the meeting, "how about we jump into the agenda and show the board the progress we've made."

"Uh, sure, great idea," I said. I clicked to the next slide and began running through what we had prepared, but my mind wasn't on the meeting.

Somehow the acquiring company was on to my strategy, using the board to get me to stop. Whoever they were, they must not know me well, because that only made me want to double down on my efforts.

Game on.

MONTH 3

CHAPTER 14

o you feel pretty confident that Massive and…what was the other one?" Charles asked.

"Codeword 9," I said.

"Right, Codeword 9, how could I forget that," Charles said, shaking his head. "So you're fairly certain that neither of those companies is trying to acquire you."

"Unless both of their CEOs are somehow exceptional actors, I can't see how it's either of them," I said.

It was just after 7 on Thursday morning and we were at the base of Foothills Mountain to, as Charles put it, "stroll up the mountain while we chat." Looking up at the incline, I was doubtful that this would feel like a stroll, at least not for me.

We began our ascent and Charles said, "You sound disappointed."

"Well, yeah, that was a total waste of time and I'm basically at square one."

"Are you sure that those meetings weren't beneficial in any way?" Charles said.

"I guess it was good to get an idea of the competition and how they operate," I said as I tried to keep up with Charles's pace. "I mean, it's always good to know the competition."

"Perhaps there's more. Think about it for a minute," he said as we came to a fork in the path. "Oh, let's take this side path, there's a great little view on the North end that most people aren't aware of."

I followed him along the path, happy that we were moving laterally for a few minutes (I could never understand how Charles always seemed to be in better shape than me despite being significantly older). What was he getting at? Sure, both Massive and Codeword 9 were larger than my agency, but they weren't trying to buy us, and, quite honestly, I was really unimpressed with both of their operations. Neither of them were leaders I wanted to emulate, and they both seemed to have turnover and culture problems.

We made our way down the path and broke through into an opening. It led to a small area with a dark green railing protecting hikers from a fairly steep drop. The view, as Charles had indicated, was spectacular.

"Wow, I've hiked this mountain a dozen times," I said, slightly exaggerating the number, "and I never knew this was here!"

"I always try to explore new areas when hiking. You know, the road less traveled, that kind of thing. You never know what you'll find. Sometimes," he said, gesturing out at the view, "you find something beautiful and totally unexpected."

"So, any more thoughts on how the meetings with those two CEOs might have benefited you?" he asked.

"Honestly, no. I know they both run large agencies in town, larger than mine in fact, but they're both…train wrecks! They don't seem to know what they're doing and their teams are both experiencing worse turnover than mine."

"You said that Codeword 9's CEO…what was his name again?" Charles asked.

"Maggs," I said.

"Right, Maggs. What was it about him that you saw as a deficiency?"

"He seems like a really nice guy, unlike Wes, but he was just all over the place. He would change his mind on decisions all the time and his team seemed to be confused about which direction they were headed. He was also completely overwhelmed and exhausted because of that, constantly going from one fire to the next."

Charles kept looking out at the open expanse and said, "So he lacked clear direction and focus."

"Exactly. I felt bad for him, actually. He wanted to do the right thing but was struggling because he didn't have a clear view of what the right thing to do was. And because he didn't, neither did his team. That is definitely holding his culture back."

"So what you're telling me," Charles said, "is that in order to build an Undeniable Culture, you have to provide a clear vision for the company. Something akin to a…"

Before he could finish, I said, "An Authentic Foundation! How did I miss that? I've literally worked on what I think the main components of an Authentic Foundation are since our last meeting. Yes, that's exactly it!"

"And is that the same thing that Wes at Massive is dealing with?" Charles asked.

"No, not entirely. I think he and his entire team know exactly what they're trying to achieve. It may not be very authentic, but they don't struggle from a lack of direction," I said.

"So what *does* he struggle with?"

"I think what surprised me the most, and I'm surprised that Wes doesn't see this—though his ego is so large I guess I get it—but he purposefully creates a dog-eat-dog, competitive culture. He told me that he struggles most with his leadership team not doing what he says, and there's a lot of infighting amongst them," I said.

"Sounds like his team doesn't trust him, or each other. Partly because they know he's really just in it for himself and could cut them at any time, but also because he breeds distrust and competitiveness to a degree that creates less of a team atmosphere and more of an individual one," Charles said.

"Right, exactly," I said.

"That sounds like another critical element in creating an Undeniable Culture, doesn't it? How can you build a culture where everyone is working together, if the team, especially the leadership team, doesn't trust each other?" he asked.

Pulling out the piece of paper and pen from my back pocket, I knelt down and added, *Step 2: Trusting Team.*

Undeniable Culture

Step 1: Authentic Foundation

1. Purpose, Vision, Tenets, and Values (PVTV)

2. Core Identity

Step 2: Trusting Team

I stood back up and put the paper and pen back in my pocket.

"Let's get back to the main path to get to the summit. But while we do, let's hike in silence and I want you to think about what you just shared with me, and how it might impact your goal of creating an undeniable culture," he said.

I followed him back to the main path and we began to hike up. There were a few tricky spots, and I was jealous of the people that passed us going down. I got a few encouraging comments from people about how we were close to the top, presumably because I was panting and sweating as I tried to keep pace with Charles. While I had done this hike a few times, I didn't remember it being so strenuous.

The top of the mountain was a long, flat expanse that allowed for a 360-degree view of the city. Even though the weather was a little chilly, it was considerably warmer given the sun bearing down on us.

Charles led us to an area on the west end where there were fewer people, put on his sunglasses—I wish I had thought of that—and said, "So, what did you come up with?"

I *had* been thinking about his question on the way up, and I thought I had it.

"First, and this goes back to what you challenged me with last time, is that to have an undeniable culture, you must have an Authentic Foundation. One that everyone understands and believes in. Per your homework assignment, I have a few things that I think are required for this. But this is what Maggs struggles with the most. His team lacks an Authentic Foundation," I said.

"Very good. And the second thing?" Charles asked.

"As I see it, while I could fill up a notepad with all the things I disliked about the way Wes runs his company, it seems to me that his biggest problem, and a key factor in creating an undeniable culture, is to have a Trusting Team," I said.

"Expand on that and tell me how it's different from having an Authentic Foundation," he said.

"It's one thing to have a foundation that is true and honest and gives everyone a roadmap for success. But if there isn't a trusting team executing on that foundation, and especially a leadership team doing so, then you'll never build the culture you want. You need everyone rowing enthusiastically in the same direction," I said.

"Bingo! See, you learned more from those two leaders than

you thought," he said. "So, what did you come up with for an Authentic Foundation?"

"Oh, right," I said, pulling a folded-up piece of paper from my back pocket. "Here is what I came up with."

I handed him the paper. He pulled his reading glasses out of his jacket pocket—the only sign I'd ever seen that he was older than me—and he unfolded the paper. It read:

Undeniable Culture

Step 1: Authentic Foundation

1. Purpose, Vision, Tenets, and Values (PVTV)

2. Core Identity

Step 2: Trusting Team

He looked at the list, and then kind of teasingly turned it over to see if there was anything else on the back.

"I know, I know, it's not a very long list," I said. "But I thought long and hard about what would need to be in place for a company to have an Authentic Foundation, and I honestly couldn't come up with anything else."

Charles smiled and said, "Well, I do like the very recent addition of 'Trusting Team' as a second step toward building an Undeniable

Culture. How about for our next meeting you take a stab at what might be required to create a trusting team.

"For now, walk me through your thinking on an Authentic Foundation."

"It seems to me," I said, "that the main thing you need is to have your PVTV, or something like it, set. A team needs to understand why the company exists and what they're working for - that's the Purpose. Then they need to know where they are headed and how they're going to get there - that's the Vision and Tenets. And the Values will show them how to behave along the way."

"Sounds familiar, go on," he again teased.

"And then beyond that, a company must have something that they stand for, like, in the scope of what they do as a business. I actually learned that from Mark, my client at RedBrick," I said. I then explained how Mark had shared with me that he would be looking for what each of our agencies—mine and Massive—stood for.

"I like that. Do you know what your company stands for?" he asked.

"Not yet, I still have to figure that out. Beyond those two things, I can't think of anything else I would add."

"I was just giving you a hard time about the list being short. I only had two things on my list, actually, but I like your second one a lot. I think in order for a business to have an Authentic Foundation, there must be a 'Doing Good' component.

"In my 30s I had a bit of a reboot to my life, and as a part of that, I began learning how to build businesses that focused on bringing the team together first and foremost. Along that journey, while building my first company, I stumbled upon the power of doing good in bonding people together. I can tell you that story later, but the gist is, when a team does good together, they build a foundation that is hard to break," he said.

"I love that, and can think of several times that we took the team to volunteer and how much everyone seemed bonded after those experiences! Can I have that paper back?"

I pulled the pen out of my back pocket and wrote *Doing Good Together* on the page:

Undeniable Culture

Step 1: Authentic Foundation

1. Purpose, Vision, Tenets, and Values (PVTV)

2. Core Identity

3. Doing Good Together

Step 2: Trusting Team

"And of course, none of this means anything if it's not true and authentic, and if you're not living them every day at your company. People won't believe in these things if they're just fancy words on a slide," he said.

"Roger that," I said. "Before we go, there's one more thing I wanted to ask you about. It's becoming clear to me that someone is leaking information about our company to whoever is trying to buy us."

I shared what happened at the last board meeting and how they knew things that they shouldn't have known.

"Hm, based on everything you've shared with me, I'm actually not surprised. But the bigger question is, so what? Are you going to let that change the journey you're on to turn the company around? And can the acquiring company really do anything to stop you?"

"I guess not," I said. "No, it won't stop me, but I do want to know who is being dishonest with me and leaking this information."

"I'm sure that will come out in due time, but I wouldn't spend much time worrying about it. You have bigger, more important things to do. Like we do, right now. That storm cloud has been getting closer and closer as we've talked, we better start heading back down," he said.

I looked around and everyone else had left the peak. Seems they had noticed the storm cloud before we did.

As we started down the path, I couldn't help but wonder if Charles knew more about my situation than he was letting on.

CHAPTER 15

"...and our Vision is to be sought-after by…shoot, what was it again?" I asked out loud, to myself. I was in our living room trying, and failing, to memorize our company's PVTV.

Sarah walked in and I said, "I haven't memorized anything since the Pledge of Allegiance in elementary school. This is tough!"

"Why do you need to do that again?" she asked. "Seems silly."

"It's important that the leader, and the leadership team, memorize the PVTV word-for-word so that we can recite it at any point."

"Uh-huh," she said, looking doubtful. She picked up the piece of paper in front of me with our PVTV written on it. "And you think you're going to get your entire leadership team to memorize this?"

"That's the plan," I said, "but first, I have to do it to show them it's possible."

"Let me guess, Charles suggested this and Paul hates it."

"Bingo, which is what makes me think I'm onto something," I said, laughing.

Just then, Danielle walked into the room. She was the cutest little thing, all dressed up for her day at school. Pigtails, unicorn lunch box, the whole nine yards.

"Weady to go!" she said in her three-year-old dialect.

It was Friday morning and we had made a habit of taking Danielle to her school together and staying for the morning assembly. We headed out the door, Sarah putting Danielle in her car and me jumping into mine. The school was only a few minutes down the road, but I needed to head straight to work after so we decided to drive separately.

The assembly was held in the gymnasium of the school. Parents sat in the bleachers and the kids sat in rows according to their grade level, with the youngest kids closest to the stage. After finding a parking spot, I made my way to the gym and eventually found Sarah toward the middle of the bleachers saving me a seat.

I was a fan of the principal of Danielle's school. He had a great vision for what he wanted the school to be, and perhaps even more impressively, he knew every single kid in the school's name and greeted them as such each morning as they entered the front door. That was definitely not a skill set I had developed yet.

The assembly began and it didn't take long for my mind to drift back to the office. Our company meeting was coming up next week and I wanted to build on the momentum from our recent offsite where we successfully developed our PVTV. I knew that creating our PVTV, while an important first step, was only the beginning of the process. We would have to find ways to bring it to life on a consistent basis, otherwise there'd be no lasting change.

Sarah elbowed me in the side and my attention snapped back to the assembly. I heard the principal say, "And as we end all of our assemblies, I'll call on any child that wants to acknowledge one of their peers for a way that they exhibited our Values throughout the week."

He handed an extra microphone to an older kid, and the two of them made their way around the floor, handing a mic to a child that wanted to recognize one of their peers.

A young girl stood up. I did the quick math, counting the rows between where she was sitting and where Danielle was sitting, and deduced that she was in the third or fourth grade. She said, "I want to acknowledge Michael because on the playground last week I fell down and he helped me up, and that was very Responsible," she said. Responsibility was one of their school Values.

I saw all the kids on her row look toward one kid, who gave a big, toothy grin and turned a bright shade of red. Sarah whispered to me, "Aw, look how happy he is that she acknowledged him."

It went on like this for 10 minutes, with child after child excitedly acknowledging one of their classmates, and the recipient of the praise beaming with pride. Eventually, the principal had to end the lovefest and get everyone to class.

Danielle waved to us as her class exited the gym and as I walked to my car, I realized I had a big grin on my face. Apparently, even I was feeling the ripple effect of the praise that the kids were giving each other. And it gave me an idea…

CHAPTER 16

"I just don't understand it. There has to be a correlation, but I can't find it."

Rachel was sitting on the couch in my office, laptop perched on her knees. She wanted to walk me through the data that she and Paul had been gathering, with the goal of showing me how our operations and processes were affecting our culture, and how the effects of that were impacting our lack of growth.

"Walk me through what you've been gathering," I said.

"Okay, so I pulled together all of our operational and project management systems, looking at how we task our team members and how work flows through the company. I then layered that next to our employee satisfaction surveys, looking at when people complained about specific things and generally when the team was unhappy," she said.

"What were you looking for in the employee complaints?" I asked.

"My gut was that in the timeframe that people complained about a certain process or experience they had at the agency, we'd see a direct correlation to client satisfaction going down. Think of it like this, if our team was unhappy in Q2, we'd likely see that our client satisfaction would go down in Q2 or maybe Q3, and that would result in a loss of revenue. Maybe the client stops working with us or stops giving us new assignments, or maybe we just perform badly and our profit and revenue drop," she said.

"That makes sense to me. And you're not seeing that?"

"No! Paul worked with Steve to gather the client surveys and together we pulled the financials, but there was never a connection…at least not as far as I can see. And I ran the numbers several times!" she said, clearly frustrated.

That was odd. The reasoning made perfect sense, and I knew Paul and Rachel were sticklers for precision, so the data was probably spot on.

"It does seem like there should be a correlation. Maybe this is one of those things that we know in our gut is correct, but we can't quite put our finger on exactly how it's happening?"

"Uh, hello, have you met me?" she asked, jokingly. "I'm not going to sleep well until I find out why this data doesn't match up. There must be something…"

Tina poked her head in the door. "Hey guys, the company meeting starts in less than five minutes, just a heads up."

"Thanks, we'll be right there," I said. I looked back at Rachel and said, "Well, if there's a correlation, I know you'll find it. For now, I need to rehearse the PVTV one more time to make sure I can say it by heart at the company meeting."

She gave a light nod of her head and kept working on her laptop. After a moment she looked up and said, "Oh, wait, you want me to leave while you do that?"

"Well, kinda, yeah," I said.

"But aren't you going to do it in front of the whole company in a few minutes? Why can't you do it while I'm here now?"

"I don't know, it feels...different. It's weird, I know, but..." I said, motioning to the door.

She sighed, grabbed her laptop, walked to the door, and said, "You're an odd one, Will, you know that right?"

I laughed and said, "I know, it's part of my charm though, right?"

As she closed the door she said with a grin, "Uh huh, you keep telling yourself that."

CHAPTER 17

"Good morning, everyone," I said, opening up the company meeting. The team had gathered in The Farm and were piled together amidst the cubicles. "I'm now going to kick off this meeting by reciting our PVTV by heart. Before I do, I should warn you that I practiced this in front of my daughter a few times and her only critique was 'not enough unicorns,' so Linda, if you and the writing team could try to workshop in some unicorns before our next meeting, that would be great."

Deep breath. Just get started. You've put in the time, you know you've got this.

"Okay, here we go. Our Purpose is to inspire happiness through positive relationships...."

Somehow, someway, I made it through the PVTV without messing up a word. To my surprise, when I finished, the team gave me a massive round of applause.

"Don't get too excited. I'm expecting all of you to be able to do that one day, and at our next company meeting someone from our leadership team will do it," I said, glancing at the leadership team. I saw the smiles disappear from their faces and a few eye rolls.

I then called Paul and Rachel up to the front so they could walk everyone through how we were doing operationally. Martha then updated everyone on a few new HR policies, and Steve talked about our client relationships, focusing on RedBrick and the upcoming RFP. After that, Ahmet gave an overview of our sales pipeline.

Once the baton was handed back to me, I said, "I have some exciting news to share. Starting next month, we're going to have a monthly Do Good event. This is where we help a local nonprofit in town, working together as a team to better our community. We'll work the time into the schedule so no one is double-booked. For this first one, everyone is required to attend, and in the future, you'll be expected to attend at least half of them."

After working with Charles on the core elements of an Authentic Foundation, I had spent time thinking about each of them. I felt like we were doing a good job so far with our PVTV, though we'd need to continue working on bringing it to life. My memorization was a first step, so I'd call that progress.

The second component, a company's Core Identity, was still a bit of a mystery. I'd circle back to that, but the third element, Do Good Together, was a bit easier. After brainstorming with Paul (which was basically me brainstorming with him as a curmudgeon during the entire process), I had landed on forming the Do Good Committee and a monthly charity experience.

Someone from the back asked, "Do we get to pick which charity we help?"

"Glad you asked! In fact, we're going to be standing up a Do Good Committee. Martha is going to coordinate getting it set up, and after that, one of you will lead it and as a group you'll make those decisions. Everyone who's interested, please reach out to Martha at the end of this meeting." I could tell there was going to be a lot of interest in that committee.

"Now, I have one more thing I want us to do with the final 10 minutes of the meeting. You all work so hard supporting one another and I'm guessing you rarely have time to share your appreciation for each other. So I thought it would be fun to spend some time acknowledging each other. I'll start, and then anyone that wants to go next just raise your hand," I said. "And if you can somehow connect your acknowledgment to our Values, even better. As a reminder, our Values are putting the team first, thinking positively, celebrating diversity, doing good, and having fun."

"I'd like to acknowledge Rachel," I said, turning toward her, "for always making sure that no matter how much we're struggling, we always look at the positive side of things and strive for a solution. Especially over the last few months, you've really done a great job keeping us focused and positive."

She beamed and, predictably, was the first to raise her hand to go next.

Standing up, Rachel said, "I'd like to acknowledge Steve and the account team for coming together and helping us with all the data that Paul and I have been collecting. I know that was a pain in the butt, but you came together and got it done."

A few more hands popped up and I started calling on people. One after another, someone would stand up and acknowledge either an individual or a group of people. As people became more comfortable with it, more hands started flying up and I realized we wouldn't be able to get to everyone before our time ran out.

"Okay, I think we have time for one more," I said, looking around the room. "Susie, you get the honor of closing us out."

Susie, typically a bit shy, practically jumped out of her seat.

"I think most of you know that this week was very hard for me." Susie's dog had passed away over the previous weekend and even I knew that she had been having a hard time with it. "I haven't been sleeping well and have had a hard time feeling like myself. Yesterday I was having an especially bad day and with back-to-back meetings, I had missed lunch altogether. At 1:30 I had a short 15-minute break and I just put my head on my desk and started to cry, probably from exhaustion as much as anything else."

Everyone was silent and I could see some tears welling up in a few eyes.

"I felt a hand start to rub my back and I turned around and it was Debbie. She sat next to me and put a bag on the table. She said she knew I was having a tough time and realized that I hadn't eaten lunch yet. She then pulled out two meals, one salad and one sandwich, and told me we were going to have lunch together. It just made me feel so supported and I loved knowing someone was thinking about me," she said.

I looked over to Debbie who was wiping tears from her eyes. Someone yelled out, "What did you choose, the sandwich or the salad?"

Everyone laughed and Susie said, "Of course I chose the sandwich!"

"That was great, thanks for sharing that with us, Susie. And Debbie, I'm not sure if I've heard a better example of 'team first' than that. I appreciate everyone who shared their acknowledgments with us today. Okay, let's get back out there."

As everyone began going back to their desks, I saw several people swing by Susie on the way out to check in on her. I had no idea that the acknowledgments would be such a huge hit. And crying? Heck, even I had trouble fighting back tears at the end there.

Thinking about it, there had never been a time in our company's history where people were given the chance to acknowledge one another. How could I have missed something so obvious?

CHAPTER 18

The next morning I arrived at the office around 10 after making a stop by The Steaming Cup to fuel up on coffee and knock out some emails. As I made my way from the lobby to my office, I could feel a new kind of energy.

Tina, who was always cheerful, seemed to have an even bigger smile on her face when she greeted me. I saw team members gathered together in various areas, and the sound of laughter echoed through the hallways.

Before entering my office, I turned and looked out at The Farm. While I couldn't quite see everyone—those dang cubicle walls were so high—I could sense that something had changed.

I opened the door to my office and found Paul sitting on the couch.

"Hey, morning," I said.

Paul looked up and said, "Hey, man."

"What's up? You look bummed out."

Paul shuffled in his seat and took a deep breath. "Well, this morning on my way into the office, I saw something that I need to share with you."

"Sure," I said, sitting down on the chair across from him, "what is it?"

"You know how I usually stop by the breakfast place around the corner?" he asked.

"Yeah, over at Colony Square." I knew the place because we'd had breakfast there many times since moving into this building.

"Right. Well, this morning when I got there I saw… Charles and James having breakfast together. There were documents on the table and they were going over what looked like financial figures. I couldn't see much because I didn't want them to see me," he said. "But I did see the name of our agency at the top of one of the pages."

"Huh, I wasn't even aware they knew each other," I said. "Maybe they're working on something together."

Paul scrunched his face up, giving me a look that seemed to say, "*Come on, man, you're really not seeing it?*"

"What?" I asked.

"Has Charles ever mentioned knowing James?" he asked.

"No," I said.

"And you don't think that's odd, especially given everything you've shared with him about the board meetings and the acquisition process?"

"Not really…"

"Will, come on. Put the pieces together. You were just telling me the other day that we have a leak, that someone is telling the board about what we're doing. Outside of our team here, and Sarah, is there anyone else who knows about this other than Charles?"

He was right. No one else on the team knew James or the board, at least not to my knowledge. Why would Charles and James be meeting together, looking at documents about our agency? And why wouldn't Charles mention their relationship? I'd specifically mentioned James to him…

"But…why would Charles be trying to help the board sell the company?"

Paul shrugged. "Why would anyone unless they're going to benefit from our sale? Maybe he's working with the acquiring company. I don't know, but the fact that he didn't tell you is a big red flag. I told you I was worried about how much you share with him."

A bit shocked, I said, "Thanks for letting me know, Paul. I need time to think about this."

Paul stood up and put his hand on my shoulder. "I'm really sorry to have to be the one to tell you about this, Will."

He left and asked if I wanted the door closed or open. I was too numb to answer, so he closed the door.

I was due to meet with Charles the next day, so I sent him a text:

Charles, sorry, I have to cancel our meeting tomorrow.

He wrote back a few minutes later:

No problem, everything ok?

Never better, I replied.

Charles had been my mentor for a few years and I felt like I could trust him completely. I had shared so much with him… how could he betray me like this?

MONTH 4

CHAPTER 19

"Should we text him or just get started?"

We were in one of the smaller conference rooms and Rachel was clearly impatient that Paul hadn't shown up to our meeting yet. I had decided to invite both of them to a meeting to work on the Trusting Team component of building an Undeniable Culture. We had waited 10 minutes past the meeting time but Paul still hadn't shown up.

"Sure, I'll text him and see where he is," I said. After I sent him the text, I asked Rachel how she thought last week's company meeting had gone.

"Will, it was mind-blowing how much better that company meeting was than any we've done in the past. Even the meeting where we announced that we were moving into this office paled in comparison. I mean, people were crying!"

"I know, I couldn't believe it. That was definitely not what I had imagined," I said.

She looked at me and said, "By the way, where did you come up with the idea to do acknowledgments? Read it in a book or something?"

"Actually, I saw it at my daughter's school and thought it might be worth a try. I had no idea it would be so powerful. I'm thinking we do it at least one more time to see if people are still into it, and if it goes even half as well as the first time, we make it a regular part of our meetings," I said.

My phone vibrated and I picked it up. Paul's text read:

sorry, stuck in another meeting, not going to make it.

"He's not coming, is he?" Rachel said, likely seeing the disappointment on my face.

"No, apparently not," I said.

"Don't take it personally, he just…doesn't get why we're making all these changes. Honestly, and you know I'm a big fan of the changes you've made so far," she said, "but I don't really understand the motivation either."

She was right to question the moves, of course. Only Paul and I knew about the possible sale of the company. And since Paul wasn't really trying to help me…

"Okay, it's time I fessed up," I said. "Now, I'm going to share something with you that I probably should have when it first happened, but I need you to make sure to keep it between us. Deal?"

"Of course, you know you can trust me. What's up?" she asked.

And then I just unloaded everything to her. The first board meeting, the decision to fight it, the meetings with the two other agencies (and the upcoming one with Brainstick), and the attempt to create an Undeniable Culture.

When I got done, she was looking at me with wide eyes and a curious expression on her face.

"Wow. Well, thanks for sharing all of that. I wish you would have looped me in earlier so I could be helping you with it. That still doesn't explain why Paul isn't on board to help. I mean, everyone knows he's not always a fan of your crazy ideas, but I would think he'd want to save the firm if given the chance," she said.

"Paul has always been more interested in selling the business than I was, and even more so lately. But what do you mean that everyone knows he isn't a fan of my ideas?" I asked.

"Well," she said, squirming a bit in her seat, "let's just say that Paul sometimes has a hard time keeping his frustrations to himself. It's never anything other than a frustrated vent, and I've never heard him do it to anyone other than leadership team members. Look, partnerships can be tough…"

I knew Paul and I weren't always on the same page, but I was shocked and disappointed to hear that he would speak out against me to other people in the company, especially the leadership team. I'd always made it a point not to let anyone on the team know that we weren't always in lockstep. It's critical for leaders to back each other up in front of the team and to be honest with each other about their issues.

"...and of course, his intentions are always to help the company, never to undermine you…"

"It's fine," I said, relieving her from the need to make me feel better about it. "Honestly, it's not a big deal. Paul and I are good, we just need to work on communicating better with each other. I probably don't do a great job of listening when we aren't seeing eye to eye. Let's go ahead and jump into the meeting, and if Paul makes it we can catch him up."

I stood up and wrote on the whiteboard:

Undeniable Culture

Step 1: Authentic Foundation

1. Purpose, Vision, Tenets, and Values (PVTV)

2. Core Identity

3. Doing Good Together

Step 2: Trusting Team

"What I want to focus on today is the second step to building an Undeniable Culture—building a Trusting Team. But first, any questions about creating an Authentic Foundation?" I asked.

"I think I get it. We've already created our PVTV and started putting it into action. And now I see why you wanted to create the Do Good Committee. Any progress so far on figuring out our Core Identity?"

I walked her through the conversation that Mark and I had, and Mark's (somewhat annoying) obsession with Chopping Blade.

"So it's their creativity that he likes?" she asked.

"He definitely likes how creative they are, but I think more to the point, he likes that they have a…thing. Something that they rally around, that everyone in their company believes they're the best at."

"Interesting. So you think it matters less what the thing is, and more that everyone believes in it?"

"Right. And as I've thought about it, I think Mark likes it because the team is focused, but I also imagine it brings the team together in ways that are much more powerful."

"And how is that different from our Purpose of Inspiring Happiness?" she asked.

"I've been thinking about that. On one hand, I think it could be the same, but it has to connect to the work the team does directly. But I can also see it being something entirely different. I haven't quite put my finger on what it could be for us. Do you have any ideas?"

She thought for a moment and said, "Nothing immediately comes to mind. Which I guess is part of the problem."

"Yes, if neither of us can quickly put our hands on something the entire team stands for, then we don't have it. Yet," I said. "Let's put a pin in that for now. I want to talk about what it takes to build a Trusting Team."

We spent the next hour brainstorming concepts. By the end, we had a whiteboard full of ideas with three core themes grouping them together.

"Okay, let's see if I can recap where we are," Rachel said. "And I think these are in order of importance, because one kind of leads to the next.

"The first thing you need if you want to create a Trusting Team is a Focused Leader. If the person calling the shots isn't someone that the team can trust, then everything falls apart. The leader must be honest with the team, set the Vision for where the company is heading, be able to make decisions, and give team members the autonomy to do their job."

"That sounds exactly the opposite of what I experienced with Maggs when I visited Codeword 9," I said. "He was all over the place, changing his mind constantly and never giving people clear direction."

"Exactly," Rachel said. She looked around the whiteboard and pointed to a note we had written. "And at the same time, the leader must be willing to admit mistakes when he or she makes them. Humility and candor are key to being a trusting leader."

"Okay, all of that lines up. Take us through the next one," I said.

She looked back up at the whiteboard and said, "Once you have a Focused Leader, you need to make sure you have a United Leadership Team. How about you walk us through this one?"

"Sure. I think where we ended up was, it doesn't matter how great the leader is, if the leadership team is not in lockstep toward the Vision, then no one else will take it seriously. A United Leadership Team is one that believes in the leader, trusts and supports one another, and are accountable—to the company, to their direct reports, but mostly, to each other," I said.

"One thing we wrote down was, 'Debate, and then Commit,' which means it's okay to question ideas and debate the solution while you're together as a leadership team, but once a decision is made, everyone has to commit to it and never waiver. If the rest of the team sees leaders presenting different ideas about how to move forward, no one knows who to follow or where the company is headed."

Patrick Lencioni's book, *The Five Dysfunctions of a Team*, is a terrific resource to work on building a trusting team.

"That's so important, and something we should do a better job of with our leadership team," I said. "I don't think we have enough of those debates. Which leads us nicely into our next theme."

"Yes, I think more than anything this next one is where we struggle the most. Once you have a Focused Leader and a United Leadership Team, you must have Active Meetings. Let's see, some of our notes on that are… People in meetings must feel that it is safe to ask tough questions, dialogue should be encouraged… oh yeah, and a meeting must have a purpose and everyone in the meeting must be required. If you aren't sure if someone should be in a meeting, they probably shouldn't be."

"And the person running the meeting should actively be trying to make all of those things happen," I added. "I agree, this is one we need to work harder on. Even in our company meetings, we probably don't make sure it's a safe place for people to ask questions."

Once again, Patrick Lencioni has a terrific book on creating better meetings, *Death By Meeting.* (It's worth buying that book simply for the title!)

Rachel took a photo of the whiteboard with her phone, erased it, and wrote:

Undeniable Culture

Step 1: Authentic Foundation

1. Purpose, Vision, Tenets, and Values (PVTV)

2. Core Identity

3. Doing Good Together

Step 2: Trusting Team

1. Focused Leader

2. United Leadership Team

3. Active Meetings

She sat back down next to me and we both looked up at the words, silent for a few minutes.

"So, what do you think?" she asked.

"I like it," I said. "I like it a lot. I can see how powerful a culture would be if it had these two components. I see weaknesses in our company when aligned with these steps, and my time with both Wes from Massive and Maggs with Codeword 9 reinforce a lot of these. Wes, in particular, is unable to create a United Leadership Team. Sure, he's much more focused than Maggs was, but he's not authentic and doesn't work hard to make sure his leadership team trusts each other and backs each other up."

I guess Charles was right when he suggested that those meetings with the agency leaders weren't wasted...

"Knock, knock," Tina said, poking her head into the room. "Just a heads up, Will, that you have to leave for your next meeting in a few minutes."

"Thanks," I said. Tina left and I walked up to the whiteboard.

"It still feels like something is missing from this," I said.

"Let me guess, because each of our steps has three core ideas associated with them, you want to consider if there's a third step because you like...symmetry," she said, laughing.

"Well, I do like a nice consistent plan," I laughed, realizing she wasn't entirely wrong. "But no, it's more than that. We have listed here a step focused on the leader and another focused on the leadership team. But it feels like there should be one focused on the entire company."

"The meeting Tina said you needed to go to is with Jane at Brainstick, right?" she asked.

I nodded.

"I wonder if you might learn something from what they're doing, right or wrong, that might help us figure out what the third step could be. That is, if you have time to observe while you're all Sherlock Holmes'ing trying to figure out if she's trying to buy us."

I laughed and said, "Good point. Speaking of which, I better head that way."

After I wrote down our final list in my notepad, Rachel took a photo of the whiteboard and then erased it. As we left the conference room, I thought about how refreshing it had been to work with her on this, and how draining my other sessions with Paul had been. I really needed to work on my relationship with him. After all, if I was going to be a Focused Leader, I needed to be on the same page with my partner.

CHAPTER 20

The Lyft ride to Brainstick's office was longer than I expected. Their office was over 30 minutes outside of the city, which was odd for an advertising agency. Being centrally located in the more active areas of town was typically a bonus when trying to attract new employees and win new clients.

Any expectations I had of their office being overly hip to offset the location were squashed as we pulled up to a fairly generic office park.

"Are you sure this is the right address?" I asked the driver, certain we were in the wrong location.

"355 Tucker Avenue," he said, looking at the map on his phone. "Suite 455. Yep, this looks like the right place."

Sure enough, as he pulled up to drop me off at the front door, I could see the Brainstick logo emblazoned on the glass door.

I hopped out, checked my watch—five minutes early, perfect—and opened the door. The reception area was fairly small, with three gray chairs, a glass coffee table, and a reception desk in the corner.

"Oh, hello," the young woman behind the desk said. "You must be Will. I'm Linda."

"That's me. I'm here to see Jane."

"Great, I'll take you back in just a minute. Would you like a bottle of water?" she asked.

"No, thanks, but I appreciate the offer." I settled into one of the seats and asked, "So, how long have you worked here?"

"Going on about six weeks," she said.

"Liking it so far?" I asked.

"You bet! I have an engineering degree and I love the way things operate around here," she said. Noticing the confused look on my face, she continued, "Oh, right, why am I working the reception desk if I have an engineering degree. Well, my father, also an engineer, knows Jane from a nonprofit board they're on together, and he told me that I should try to do anything possible to get a job here. Jane is known for promoting people if they perform, so I decided to give it a shot."

That was a good quality to have in a leader. It made me wonder what role Tina, our receptionist, might want to move into.

Linda's phone buzzed and her entire desk vibrated. "Sorry," she said, embarrassed. "This desk is a bit rickety and I always forget to keep my phone in my purse. That was a note from Jane, she's ready for you. I'll take you back."

She led me through the door into a long hallway. It appeared to go all the way down to the back of the building. We passed door after door with name plates on each of them.

Bill Fisk

Account Management

Flint Marko

Creative Lead

Felicia Hardy

Risk Management

On and on it went, and in each office I could hear keyboard keys being pounded or someone on the phone, yet all the doors were closed. It felt odd to be in an agency's office and have such little… energy. There wasn't even any local art or predictable posters on the wall. Instead, we passed five straight years of Best Places to Work awards (as impressive as it was confusing based on what I'd seen so far) and that was it.

"Is there a main, open area where a lot of people work? At our office we have something we call The Farm, which, I know, kind of an awful name, but one of our creatives came up with it and it kind of stuck. It's where most of our team sits. Anything like that here?" I asked.

"As a matter of fact, we do. And," she said as we took a turn to the right, "here it is."

In front of me was a massive conglomeration of the highest-walled cubicles I had ever seen. It looked like a little business city, with hallways cutting through it from one end to the other. Everyone had their own cubicle, almost like a small personal office. I saw one guy walking across the room, but otherwise I couldn't see another person even though the room was full.

"This is where all of our production team works, including the engineers, which I hope to join soon," she said. "Come on, Jane's office is right over here."

She led me through Cubicle City and around two more turns until we ended up at a corner office.

Jane T.
CEO and Founder

Linda knocked, and I heard Jane say, "Come on in." Linda opened the door and I stepped through.

Jane T. (I actually didn't know her last name, only ever seeing it written that way) was about average height, had blonde hair pulled back in a tight bun, and was very fit. To back that up, I saw a few pictures of her running in what appeared to be major marathons on the wall behind her.

"Will, great to meet you," she said, extending her hand. We shook hands and she motioned for me to have a seat at one of the chairs in front of her desk.

Linda exited, closing the door softly.

"She's great," I said, motioning to the door. "And she said she's excited to one day be an engineer here, assuming she does a good job as a receptionist. If it helps, I'd say she's doing a great job there."

Jane smiled and said, "Linda sure is great, and yes, I plan to promote her next month."

"I think it's great that you have that mindset. I'm sure it inspires people to do their best."

She looked at me a bit skeptically and said, "It does, but you know the real reason I do that, right?"

Based on the expression she was giving me, I felt like I should know. Luckily, before I could admit my ignorance, she continued.

"Think of it like this. If I hired a junior engineer, I'd have to pay them at least $60,000. Probably closer to $70,000. And that's what Linda could get out on the market at another firm, I'm sure of it. Instead, by starting her as a receptionist at $35,000, I not only get to make sure she's a good fit for our business, kind of like a test run, but also, when I make her a junior engineer and give her a $10,000 raise, she'll think it's the greatest day of her life. Plus, she'll be so thrilled to do the work she really wants to do, she'll be content at that salary for a solid year. It will take her three to four years to get to $70,000. She'll be happy the entire time, so it's a win-win."

"Wow, that's…smart," I said, not quite sure how to react. I guess it made sense, Linda would be happy, but didn't she deserve to be paid what she's worth?

"So, your note said you wanted to meet because you're on some kind of journey to get to know the other agency CEOs?" she asked.

"Right, I just thought, why not get to know the other leaders in our industry and see if we can learn some things from each other, maybe even help each other out if the situation is right?" I said.

"And have you met with any of the others yet?" She asked, again looking a little skeptical.

"I've met with two others: Maggs from Codeword 9 and Wes from Massive."

"What did you think about them? I think I met Maggs once, but never Wes. Heard about him, though," she said.

"Oh, I liked them, but boy are they different. Their offices did have one thing in common though, actually, but yours is designed in a different way," I said.

"What's that?"

"Well, the layout of your space is," I said, trying to pick the right words, "more closed off and private."

She nodded, "I like to describe it as 'efficient.' But yes, I get what you mean. I went to an industry event at the Codeword 9 office, that's when I briefly met Maggs, and it was held in the middle of their office in that big open area. Honestly, I don't know how people get any work done in an environment like that."

"I'm sure it can be a bit chaotic when you have everyone in the same area without any walls or cubicles, but I bet it helps the creative process and allows the team to get to know each other and build trust," I said.

She gave me a smile that didn't look all that sincere, almost like she was smiling at a seven-year-old who just said something adorably ignorant. "Yes, I've read the same books you have that talk about the importance of letting team members build trust, and over-sharing with them, and yada yada yada. Maybe it's my engineering background, but I've always thought of my team members as billable resources that, if I can manage them as effectively as possible, with the fewest distractions, they'll produce optimal results for the company," she said.

Turning her chair to face the large monitor behind her, she said, "Let me show you something." She typed on the keyboard for a moment, clicked on a few tabs in her browser, and popped up a massive spreadsheet.

"This graph is a year-by-year view of how billable our team is. See this big jump in productivity?" she asked, pointing toward the middle of the graph.

Indeed, there was a significant jump in the numbers where she was pointing. I nodded.

"This is when I decided to change up the structure of our office to be more 'closed off,' as you called it. More personal offices, less opportunities for people to talk around the proverbial water cooler, things like that. I even replaced our old cubicles with ones that had the highest walls in the market, so people could have their own personal space and be less likely to chit-chat and become distracted during the day," she said.

"Wow, that's a remarkable uptick in productivity!" I said. "I'm sure if there were any team members on the fence when you made these changes, they quickly embraced the concept when they saw this data."

She gave me that look again. "Will, I don't share this kind of information with the team. In fact, I try to share as little as possible with them when it comes to our numbers and how we operate. I'm trying to create the most efficient business in the industry, and the more they're distracted by things that don't concern them, the less likely they'll perform at their best."

Interesting. Was it possible the path I was on by creating our PVTV and making sure it was woven into our entire company would ultimately just distract everyone? I needed to think that through more, perhaps I was rushing into this… Checking my watch, I realized we didn't have much time and I had yet to assess whether or not Jane was the one trying to buy our shop.

"Makes a lot of sense," I said. "I was curious about your stance on acquisitions. I know a while back you acquired another shop. How did that go?"

"Well, let's see. How can I put this in just the right words? Oh yes, it was a complete and unmitigated *disaster,*" she said, turning the monitor off and swiveling her chair back to me. "It was the first time I had gone through the process and I sincerely hope it's the last time. The entire exercise was a huge distraction to both of our firms, the integration went terribly, and the CEO, whom I ignorantly made president of our agency after the acquisition, bailed on me after just six months. Why, are you considering acquiring an agency? Honestly, I can't think of anything more helpful to share with you today than this—don't do it!"

While I didn't share her belief that acquisitions are to be avoided at all costs, I was relieved that she wasn't the one trying to acquire us. It felt like she was building more of a factory than a creative agency and I had the feeling she'd be a tough CEO to work for. Effective maybe, but tough.

"No, not at all," I said, "but thanks for the advice. Sorry the former CEO bailed, that must have been tough."

Remembering my walk through her office, I said, "But at least through that period it seems like you've managed to keep the culture up, what with all the Best Places to Work awards I saw in the hallway."

"That impresses you?" she asked, seeming genuinely curious.

"Well, yeah," I said, wondering why that would even be a question. "It means you have a place where people love working."

"Does it? Or does it mean that a group of judges created a list of things that they think make a great place to work, and I was able to reverse-engineer their process to figure out what to focus on? The first few years we didn't make the list, but once I broke their code, I was able to make sure we would get good marks on the things the judges liked, and ever since we've been at the top of the list."

Yikes, she really was ruthlessly robotic about how she ran her business. Hard to argue with the results, though.

I then told her a little about our shop, keeping it mostly to generic details and not letting her know about the current reshaping of our culture—which I'm sure she would have thought was a huge waste of time. Now that she opened my eyes to running a more efficient company, maybe some of it was a waste of time?

I was only a few minutes into my overview when there was a soft knock on Jane's door. After Jane said for the person to come in, Linda poked her head in the door and told her that her next appointment had arrived.

We shook hands, agreed to do this more often, and Linda walked me back through the office to the lobby. I tried to envision our office being structured like this. It was a complete 180-degree change from what I had previously thought was the right way to structure our office, but they did seem to be doing well with it.

The bigger issue, on the other hand, remained unchanged. With just over two months until the final board meeting, I was no closer to finding out exactly who was trying to buy my company out from under me. Three different visits with three different agency leaders had come up empty.

CHAPTER 21

"Will, are you insane?!"

Rachel was sitting across from me in the conference room we had met in earlier, looking at me like I had just told her that I had watched *Silence of the Lambs* with my three-year-old.

"What do you mean?" I asked, unsure what Rachel was even talking about. I had just updated her on my meeting with Jane, thinking we'd start to game plan how to mimic some of the things she was doing.

"Brainstick is the absolute last agency we'd ever want to model our business after! According to what I've heard, and this is from many people, including some of our team members, they have the highest turnover of any agency in the city! I mean, sure, Codeword 9 and Massive have that issue, but no one has it worse than Brainstick. And after you left for the meeting, I checked their ranking on Glassdoor, and let's just say Jane must not have figured out how to game that system because they have a terrible ranking and even worse reviews," she said.

"Jeez, I had no idea. I mean, my gut told me that she wasn't building an inclusive place to work—the numerous private offices, the high-walled cubes, not wanting to share information with anyone—but I shrugged it off seeing that they have solid numbers and seem to win 'Best Places to Work' every year," I said.

"I'm sure with their efficiency-focused operating model that they've become really good at the hiring process…I can't even imagine how many people they must hire a quarter in order to offset the number of people leaving."

"What a nightmare that would be. And can you believe how they manipulate the Best Places to Work award? That's nuts."

She looked at me incredulously.

"What?" I asked.

"You must know," she said, "that we do that as well. Maybe we're not as formulaic as they are about it, but we absolutely try to make sure that the things we focus on help us win the award. Remember when we started doing 'Thirsty Thursdays'?"

"Yeah, those were fun in the beginning. We had that drink station set up in the lobby and Tina would play bartender. They petered out after a while, as I recall," I said.

"Well, we only did that because one of the questions on the Best Places to Work application was, 'How many times a month does your team get together for a social outing?' Martha had suggested it as a way to make sure we had at least four such outings a month," she said.

"That's right! I do remember that. I wonder what else we do that's similar to Brainstick," I said.

Rachel stood up and walked to the whiteboard. "You said something earlier and I made a note. You said that Brainstick isn't a very inclusive place to work. Can you tell me more about what you meant?"

As I talked, she wrote on the whiteboard our earlier progress.

Undeniable Culture

Step 1: Authentic Foundation

1. Purpose, Vision, Tenets, and Values (PVTV)

2. Core Identity

3. Doing Good Together

Step 2: Trusting Team

1. Focused Leader

2. United Leadership Team

3. Active Meetings

"Everything about their environment felt too...sterilized. There was no focus on relationship building—either from the company to the team, or team member to team member—and in fact, a deliberate focus to stop relationships from happening. Communication was restricted, and heck, she even scoffed at the idea of Values being anything a company could really embrace," I said.

"And you'd agree that all of those things lead to a less-than-appealing culture, correct?" Rachel said, leading the witness.

"That's right. She might be getting financial results, but clearly their culture is suffering."

Rachel nodded and turned to look back at the whiteboard. "So, we currently have two ways to create an Undeniable Culture. The first is to create an Authentic Foundation, one in which a PVTV is created and brought to life, where the company has a Core Identity, meaning something they really stand for, and they must Do Good Together. The second component is to build a Trusting Team. For that, we know we must have a Focused Leader, a United Leadership Team, and Active Meetings.

"It sounds like what you've learned at Brainstick is that there also must be a..." she paused, tapping the dry erase marker to her chin, "let's see how this feels."

She added to the board:

Step 3: Inclusive Environment

She sat down and we were both silent for a moment.

"An Inclusive Environment...," I said, trying it out for size. "Maybe we should talk about what the components of that would be to see if it works. Hand me that marker."

Rachel tossed me the marker and I walked up to the board.

"For an environment to be inclusive, where everyone is accepted and heard, it feels like you need to have open communication. People need to know that their voice is important, and the company needs to share as much as possible so that the team understands where they fit and how they can help," I said. I wrote down, 'Open Communication,' on the board.

Rachel said, "I like that. Also, if the Values truly are important, I think that needs to be there. Something about bringing the Values to life. Maybe, 'Live the Values?'"

"I love that," I said, and wrote 'Live the Values' on the whiteboard. "Do you think that conflicts with having PVTV under an Authentic Foundation?"

She sat back for a moment, thinking. "No, I think it simply reinforces and makes having a PVTV stronger. Seems like being specific about bringing the Values to life is key."

"It's funny, I can't remember how it came up but when I was talking with Jane and the idea of Values was mentioned, she said that she thought Values were just something business leaders made up to give themselves a pass for making their teams work harder, and that she'd never met a Value that could produce a billable hour."

"In my experience there are a lot of leaders out there like that," Rachel said, shaking her head. "They either can't be bothered to work on their company's culture, or like Jane, they don't believe it's important."

"Sad, but true. What else do you think could fit with creating an Inclusive Environment?" I asked.

"Let's see, if you have Values that are truly lived and brought to life, and you're focused on ensuring Open Communication, then maybe the final piece of the puzzle is something about relationships. We should be striving for truly genuine relationships, in which people actually care about each other, right?"

I wrote "Genuine Relationships" on the whiteboard and sat back down.

Undeniable Culture

Step 1: Authentic Foundation

1. Purpose, Vision, Tenets, and Values (PVTV)

2. Core Identity

3. Doing Good Together

Step 2: Trusting Team

1. Focused Leader

2. United Leadership Team

3. Active Meetings

Step 3: Inclusive Environment

1. Live the Values

2. Open Communication

3. Genuine Relationships

"What do we think?" I asked.

"I'll want to sit on it for a while, but…I really like it," she said, and the smile on her face told me she was excited about the work we'd done.

I liked it as well, and really wished I could bounce it off Charles. But it was nice to have Rachel to work with on this. Why hadn't I involved her in these kinds of important discussions before?

CHAPTER 22

As the rest of the week rolled on, I started to notice that the new sense of energy I felt after the company meeting was starting to dissipate. People were falling back into their old routines, sticking to their cubicles or closing their office doors.

I suppose I should have expected this to happen. Announcing changes is important, but executing on those changes is ultimately all that matters.

Just then, Paul and Steve bolted through my office door.

"Will, check your email," Steve said. "The RedBrick RFP just came in."

A few clicks of my mouse later and there it was, the RedBrick RFP. I opened it up and began skimming through it.

"I think we have a really good shot at it," Paul said. "There's only one issue..."

"IT'S DUE IN ONE WEEK?!" I shouted. "This can't be right. Are you sure we just received this?"

"Oh, it wasn't a mistake. I checked with a guy on the team I know pretty well, and he told me confidentially that Mark wanted to see how each of the agencies, Massive and us, did thinking on our feet. The good news," Steve said, "is that they're compensating both of us for the work we'll have to do."

In the marketing and advertising industry, most brands ask agencies to do a significant amount of work to try to win their business. There can only be one winner, and often five or six agencies that don't win. Those agencies spend a lot of time, effort, and money in order to properly pitch the business, only to be left with nothing when the process is over. The more enlightened clients paid the agencies for their time. It was rare, but it did happen.

"That's good, and I'm not surprised, Mark is a standup guy," I said. "Well, we've always been good under pressure. What's the plan?"

We spent the next hour walking through the RFP and figuring out how we were going to tackle it. It wouldn't be easy, but I felt like we had a fighting chance, and that's all I could ask for. It was also good to see Paul excited again, and I wondered if this pitch process would reinvigorate him.

CHAPTER 23

The next day was our Do Good Day, and any hope I had that Paul might be ready to support the changes I was making were dashed when I received a text from him a few minutes before we were ready to start.

sorry, not gonna make it. unfortunately…

I didn't bother reading whatever excuse I was sure he made up to get out of coming. He was the loudest voice in our Leadership Team meeting advocating for us to reschedule given the fast deadline of the RedBrick RFP, but I made the final decision to keep the event. I was sure our team would still be able to give their best effort on the pitch, and I suspected that we might even produce a better response after everyone spent time giving back together.

I told them all this first event was required, and as far as I could tell, he was the only one who wasn't here. I needed to have a real conversation with him and figure out how to get us on the same page. I'd been procrastinating on doing that, but this was getting ridiculous. That, however, was for another day. Today, it was time to do some good.

The Do Good Committee had decided we would go to the Foothills Community Garden for our day of service. It was a nonprofit that provided small plots of land for community residents to set up a garden. Many of the people who were given the plots were struggling to make ends meet, and some were even experiencing homelessness.

A lot of maintenance was required to keep the garden in good working order, and personally I was thankful that we were going to be getting our hands dirty, literally and figuratively.

A woman who worked at the garden came out and explained what we'd be doing. There were four stations - raking and pulling weeds, hauling excess vegetation and scraps, resoiling designated areas, and running water lines. She broke us into four groups and explained that we'd rotate between the four stations over the next five hours.

After a few hours, the sun rose directly overhead and, with the temperature rising and people beginning to sweat, I grabbed Martha and we headed to my car. I had several coolers stuffed with bottled water packed in the trunk. I grabbed a cooler, and Martha and I began walking through the gardens handing out water.

After we hit the first group and were making our way to the next one, Martha stopped us and said, "Take a look at everyone for a minute and tell me what you see."

I put the cooler down and scanned the team. People were working hard, yes, and were dirty and sweating, but they were also…happy.

"Looks like a bunch of happy people, doesn't it?" she said, beating me to the punch. "It's been a while since I've seen them like this. Everyone is getting along, no bickering, and they're working together as a real team."

I nodded and said, "I do see it. And it feels different from the offsite we had two months ago at the arcade."

"I was just thinking that. This feels more…genuine. Like, the combination of working hard together in order to help other people is drawing them together in a new way. I think we're onto something with this Do Good initiative," she said.

"That is," I said, noticing someone from the next team teasing us by looking at their watch and miming drinking a water bottle, "if we can keep them hydrated so they don't pass out all over this garden! Let's get these waters to the team!"

CHAPTER 24

I was in the kitchen lacing up my running shoes when Danielle came around the corner. She saw me, her face lighting up, and she ran and hugged my leg.

"Whoa, there, where'd you come from? I thought you were sleeping!" I said. Last night she had a bad dream and, breaking every parenting book's rules for how to properly parent, we decided to let her get into bed with us. I thought I had done a good job sneaking out of bed to go for my run.

"I just woked up," she said, rubbing her eyes. "What day is it, Daddy?"

"It's Saturday, honey," I said, knowing that the information wouldn't mean anything to her. She asked what day of the week it was every morning because it made her feel grown up. I picked her up and put her in my lap and said, "Well, I'm sorry if I woke you up. I tried to be so quiet! I'm going to sneak out to go on a run, would you like me to set you up on the couch with some of your toys?"

She smiled and nodded. I carried her to the couch and grabbed a few blankets from the basket in the corner. I piled them all around her and, noticing that we hadn't cleaned up her toys off the floor before going to bed, grabbed a few and put them in her lap.

"Okay, now if you need anything, go get Mommy. I'm sure she'll be up in a few minutes, but if you can let her sleep a little bit longer I bet she'd really like that," I said.

As she started playing with one of her dolls, I went to grab my earbuds and realized that I had left them in the closet in our bedroom. Shoot! There's no way I could go back in there and risk waking Sarah up. I typically preferred to listen to an audiobook when I ran, preferably a memoir of a competitive athlete (and a bonus if it was by a competitive runner). I always felt like it was easier to complete my four-mile run when listening to someone that was training for, and actually competing in, a 26.2-mile marathon.

Alas, it wasn't meant to be, so I gave Danielle a quick kiss on the head and another reminder to try not to wake Mommy up, and I silently exited through the front door.

It was 6:30 and the sun was just starting to rise. The crisp morning weather was just what I preferred for my runs—between 50 and 60 degrees and clear skies. Taking that first step outside, I recalled something that Charles taught me in one of our first meetings.

"Will," he said, "you must realize that the hardest aspect of anything you want to accomplish is the actual starting of it. Think about exercise. Lacing up your shoes and driving to the gym, or stepping outside for a run, or getting on the floor for that first pushup, that's the hardest thing to do. Most people never get to that point. You must 'begin the begin,' as I like to say."

Being a certified creature of habit, any time I went out for a four-mile run I ran the exact same course. Two miles out and two miles back. My friends who also run always give me flak about that. *Why don't you change it up? How can you run the same course over and over again?* But to me, there's a sense of familiarity that makes the run easier, allowing me to gauge how I'm doing at each checkpoint in my head.

As I ran without the distraction of an audiobook in my ears, my mind began to drift…

I was fairly certain that none of the agencies I had visited were trying to acquire us, which also meant I was nowhere in terms of figuring out who was trying to buy my company. Actually, that wasn't entirely true. Paul had said he saw Charles meeting with James, our board chair, and it appeared they were discussing our agency. So, somehow Charles was involved…

I knew at some point I would have to talk to Charles, if for nothing else than to break off our mentor-mentee relationship. I wondered if I could do it without telling him the truth. I don't know how I could look him in the face and tell him that I knew he was being dishonest with me. That kind of confrontation was difficult for me. I'd much prefer to make up an excuse as to why I didn't need to meet with him any longer.

I made it to the top of the hill—checkpoint one—and felt pretty good, so I began to pick up the pace. As I had gotten older, I knew I needed to be checking in on my body throughout my runs. If my calf or hamstring started to hurt, for instance, I knew myself well enough to know it was time to stop. I'd run through pain a few times over the last year and ended up hobbled for weeks, so now I just shut it down when I feel pain to avoid long-term injury.

I rounded the corner, arriving on the street that would take me to the point where I'd turn around to head back home, and my mind started to wonder again…

The board meeting, the last one before the big decision, was on Monday morning. I had to work over the weekend on the presentation, but the leadership team had given me all the data I needed so it shouldn't be too hard. Paul had asked half-heartedly if he could help with it, but I told him I could put it together without him. I still hadn't brought myself to talk with him either. What was wrong with me? Why was I avoiding these tough conversations?

Aside from the basics that I would show the board—revenue and profit numbers, business development pipeline, including an update on the RedBrick RFP, and client relationship updates—I would need to give them an indication of how things were progressing within the agency. Since they knew I was trying to "fix" our company, I would need to give them confidence that it was working.

And it was working, wasn't it? And while it wasn't consistent yet, people did seem happier in spurts and I had to believe the Do Good event at Foothills Community Garden had made a difference. But no, there hadn't been enough time yet to make a significant impact.

Well, I'd have two months after the next board meeting to make sure things were improving, and improving enough for the board to notice. I felt confident about the three major components that Rachel and I had landed on for building an Undeniable Culture, so we'd have to be diligent about bringing those components to life.

I reached the turnaround and did another check on my body - everything was feeling great, take *that* old age—and I began to head back home.

I finished the run in about the time I had expected, and walked a few loops around the cul-de-sac to cool down. As quietly as I could, I opened the front door and immediately smelled the unmistakable waft of bacon. I closed the door and Danielle came running up to me and said, "Mommy woked up, and she's making bweakfast!"

Entering the kitchen, I looked at Sarah and said, "Oh, you woked up, did you?"

She laughed and said, "Yes, it was the funniest thing, I woke up right at the same time I felt a little hand patting me on the face asking, 'Mommy, are you awaked?'"

CHAPTER 25

The importance of today's board meeting was not lost on me: it was the last one before the big decision, when I'd find out if I was going to keep my company or if they were going to sell us to… well, I still haven't figured that part out.

As board members shuffled in, I greeted them and we caught up with basic chit-chat. James was enjoying the weather, Samantha's son was performing in a college musical next week, and Bruce was concerned about the lack of proper parking facilities in the city.

Bouncing between them, I saw Paul enter, say hi to a few of them, and make his way over to me.

"Hey, Will, ready for the meeting?" he asked.

"Yep. How's the proposal for RedBrick coming along?" I asked. In the early stages of a proposal or pitch process, after we decided on the overall strategy, Paul usually made sure that the team was resourced properly and that timelines were being met. I'd plug in at key points to weigh in on creative and ensure we were still on point with the strategic direction.

"So far, so good," he said, and looked at his watch. "Looks like we better get them seated so we can start the meeting."

I let everyone know it was time to start and, once they were seated, I kicked things off. The first hour of the meeting was the standard updates, and we spent about 10 minutes discussing our approach to the RedBrick assignment.

"At this point, I have to bring up the elephant in the room," I said. "I want to give you all an update on how things are progressing at the agency in terms of righting the ship, and I want to give you a chance to update Paul and me on how your process with the potential acquirer is progressing."

I could literally feel the room tighten up. This was not a conversation they were comfortable with, but so what, they were the ones who had started the process. I had no problem making them a little uncomfortable.

"We've been working hard to…retool our business, starting with our culture and team. And there have been some pleasant surprises along the way. The vibe in the office is noticeably better and the team seems to be working together more effectively. Overall, and while I'll admit there is a lot more work to be done, I'm pretty happy with the improvements we've made since our last meeting," I said.

"Mmmm, I don't know if I'd agree with that entirely," I heard Paul say, not believing my ears.

Samantha said, "What do you mean, Paul?"

"Well, I have to give Will credit, he's trying some new things. But at this point, I think the only thing we can really say is that they're new. They're not working, at least not as far as I can see, and actually you probably noticed our billable time was lower over the last month, and that's a direct result of a big team outing that Will orchestrated, resulting in the entire office being non-billable for the day," he said.

"Not the entire company," I said, giving Paul a look and trying to remind him with my eyes that he, in fact, did not attend the Do Good event.

"The point is, I don't think we're at a point where we can say any of this is working. If you ask me, it's more of a distraction than anything else. The same way you meeting with those other agencies has been a distraction," Paul said, looking at me.

Great, thanks, Paul. I wasn't planning on telling them about my covert meeting with the other agencies.

James turned to me and said, "What's he talking about, Will?"

I had no choice but to explain to the group that I had met with Codeword 9, Massive, and Brainstick, in order to see if I could figure out which of them is trying to buy us.

"I wish you had told us you were going to do that," James said. "We could have told you that we learned recently that it's not another agency. It's a private equity firm. We still don't know exactly who they are, but we get the sense there are some local people involved."

Right, I'm sure you don't know who's involved. I thought about straight-up asking him about Charles, but decided against it. No need to tip my hand that I knew.

Samantha said, "And Will, we really do believe that they have your and the company's best interests at heart. James, show him the text."

James looked at Samantha and gave an audible sigh, and said, "Sure, why not. The person we've been communicating with—mostly by text which has been an odd process for us—sent me this when I asked what their real goal was for the acquisition."

He walked over to me and held out his phone. Before looking at the text, I glanced at the top of the text string to see what the name of the person was, but it only said, Unknown.

The text chain started from James and read:

James: *I want to make sure your intentions are not to dismantle the agency after the sale. These are good people and we want to make sure they are treated well. Plus, Will and Paul have worked extremely hard over the years and we want to make sure they are taken care of.*

Unknown: *of course. and i assure you that will and paul will be taken care of*

James: *That's great, thanks.*

Unkown: *no problem*

"Thanks for showing me that," I said. "And I appreciate what you wrote. If the sale should go through, I hope you know that I will cooperate and be a positive part of the process. But until that point, I hope you can appreciate that I'm going to fight to make that choice as hard as possible for you."

I looked around the room and decided I needed to make sure there was still a chance of saving my business.

"I need your word on two things. First, that you haven't already made up your mind and simply aren't telling me. I believe in the work that we're doing to get our company back on track, even if some don't," I said, giving Paul a sideways glance. "Do I have your word that the decision hasn't been made yet?"

James said, "Of course, I can assure you that we haven't made a decision yet."

"Great," I said. "The second thing I want you all to agree to is that you'll come to the next board meeting with an open mind. I plan to take the next two months to show you that we should all be in this for the long term, together, and selling now would be a mistake. But I can't do that if you don't come with the right mindset and an openness to hearing me out. Is that fair?"

Everyone around the room nodded, and Bruce said, "We'll be excited to see what you have come up with by the next meeting. Right, James?"

James paused for a moment and I could tell he wasn't in total agreement. Then he said, "We know how much you two love this business and we will give you every opportunity to change our mind. But I need you to know that if we had to vote today, I'm pretty sure it would be a unanimous vote to sell. I want to be honest with you on that point. You've got your work cut out for you, just please don't derail the business while doing that work."

"Agreed," I said. That was about all I could ask for, and I thought it was a good way to end the meeting.

We said our goodbyes and I was hoping Paul would stay in the conference room so we could talk about what just happened, but he quickly exited along with the board members. Oh well, I'd get to him eventually. I knew he was conflicted about this process and I certainly hadn't done a good job of including him.

I packed up my things—laptop, connection dongle, notepad, and pen—and exited the conference room. Pausing for a second in the lobby, I took a deep breath and wondered to myself:

Can I really do this?

MONTH 5

CHAPTER 26

I was flipping through the final draft of the RedBrick proposal when my phone buzzed. It was a text from Charles:

Hey Will, I hadn't heard from you in a while and was wondering when the next time we could meet up.

What's the problem, Charles, running out of intel to share with the board? No thanks, pal.

I tried to think of what to write back to push him off longer, without tipping my hand that I was upset with him.

Good to hear from you, but I'm slammed at the moment.

No, that's too weak and leaves the door open. How about something a little stronger…

I'm still healing from the surgery to remove the knife from my back and I'm not up for seeing visitors.

That felt right, but probably a little too strong.

Steve popped his head into my office and said, "How's it looking, boss? Think we're ready to send it off to print?"

"Yep, come on in, I was just reviewing it," I said. I looked down at my phone and wrote:

Sorry, been slammed. This week isn't good.

Short, simple, to the point. That should push him off without raising his antennae.

I set the phone down and picked the proposal back up. "It's really strong, Steve. You and the team did a great job."

"Thanks! I really think so as well. Probably the best proposal we've produced. It tells a great story, answers all of their questions, and clearly presents the case that we're the best shop for them to choose. I can't imagine Massive can put together anything better," he said.

"I agree, it's terrific. The one thing that I still wish we had was a notion of our Core Identity," I said.

"Core Identity? What's that?" he asked.

I realized that Steve hadn't yet been a part of the brainstorming I had been doing—first with Charles, now with Rachel—and had no idea what I was talking about.

"Oh, it's something that I've been working on that I believe is critical for a company to have what I'm calling an Undeniable Culture. I'm going to be walking you and the leadership team through it at our meeting on Monday. Basically, it's what your company stands for. Mark had mentioned wanting to know what that was for both us and Massive, but I don't quite have it yet," I said.

"Huh," Steve said, scratching his chin. "Is that different from our PVTV? You saw we put that into the document, right?"

"Good question, but yes, it's different from PVTV. Our Purpose is the reason we exist, outside of the work we do. Our Purpose is to…," I stopped, waiting for Steve to finish the sentence.

"To inspire happiness!" he said.

"Nice! Yes, our Purpose is to inspire happiness. It's our reason for being. Our Vision is the company we want to be, our Tenets are how we will achieve our Vision, and our Values describe how we will behave. And all of that, our PVTV, is core to who we are as a business. Our Core Identity is separate, and it should describe what we stand for," I said.

He pointed behind me and said, "Ah, so that's what you have on that whiteboard. I noticed it when I came in."

I turned around and realized that indeed the work Rachel and I had been doing was on the rolling whiteboard that I brought in for our last brainstorming meeting.

"Yep that's it. As I said, I'll be walking you guys through it in the next leadership meeting, but for now, this proposal is terrific and I think it's ready to ship."

Steve, being a good salesman and knowing that when you get a "yes" you should get out of the meeting, stood up and headed out. I was about to ask him a question when my phone buzzed.

It was a text from Charles that read:

Will, I know something is up so I'm heading over there. Be there in five minutes.

Crap.

CHAPTER 27

Four minutes later, Tina popped her head in the door and said, "Hey, Charles is here to see you. I didn't see anything on your calendar…"

"It's okay, it's more of a random catch-up. Please send him back," I said. I still wasn't sure what I would say to him, or how I would say it. As a bit of a father figure to me, I wasn't sure I could be as direct as I needed to be. Best to start off nice and cordial, then let him know that I was aware he'd been deceiving me, and then thank him for being my mentor over the years and send him on his way.

Or maybe I could just not tell him the truth and tell him I was a big boy now and didn't need a mentor?

Perhaps I could feign laryngitis. I started clearing my throat aggressively to make my voice sound raspy, just in case the laryngitis strategy won out, when Lisa poked her head in.

"Uh, Will, everything alright?" she asked before opening the door all the way.

"Oh, yes, sorry, was just coughing a little," I said. "You can let him in."

She opened the door and Charles came through. I was always impressed by how, as a man in his late 50s or early 60s (I honestly had no idea exactly how old he was), he was in such great shape. He was wearing cycling gear and was holding his helmet in one hand and a water bottle in the other.

Tina said, "Okay, I'll leave you two to it. Charles, great to see you again."

Charles smiled and said, "Great seeing you also, Tina, and thanks for the water."

Tina left and Charles came over to me and we shook hands. Before I could ask him to take a seat, he noticed the rolling whiteboard behind me.

"Wow," he said, "you've taken our idea and really run with it!"

Shoot! I should have turned that around before he came in.

"Uh, yeah, well, I grabbed Rachel and we started working on it…"

He stood in front of the whiteboard for a few minutes and then said, "This is really, really great stuff! You should work with Rachel more often—sounds like you two make a good team. How about Paul, did he help with this?"

"Not so much. He hasn't really been into this kind of thing."

Charles turned to me and, frowning, said, "Is that why you're struggling? I can tell by your texts that something is wrong, and it's not like you to blow off our meetings. I mean, I know you're under a lot of pressure, but you know I'm always here for you…"

"Are you? Are you really always here for me?" I blurted out. I could feel that I was starting to lose control, my voice wavering. "Seems to me that maybe you're sometimes here for me, but sometimes against me."

"Will," Charles said, visibly shocked, "what in the world are you talking about?"

"I know you've been meeting with James and sharing our plans with him so the board would know what we're up to," I blurted out.

Charles, still looking stunned, said, "Now, why would I do something like that?"

"Well, Paul thinks maybe you are involved in the sale and have something to gain from it," I said.

"Oh, Paul thinks that, does he?" he said. He walked over to the couch and sat down. He took a deep breath in, exhaled, and said, "And, did he tell you why he believes that?"

"He saw you meeting with James in the cafe around the corner! Do you deny it?"

"No, I don't deny it. Do you want to ask me why I was meeting with James?"

Well, that did seem like a place I should have started.

"Sure, why were you meeting with James?" I asked, acting as if I already knew the answer so it didn't matter what he said.

"James is on the FootHills Park Committee that I told you about. He was a part of the original committee 20 years ago, and we're planning the big celebration," he said.

"Why didn't you ever tell me that you had a relationship with James?" I asked.

"First of all, I probably had told you that I knew him in the past. In fact, I know several of your board members. But when we meet and talk, I keep my personal relationships out of it so I can be a true, unbiased mentor to you," he said.

"Well, that doesn't explain how Paul saw our company name on one of the papers you and James were looking at," I said.

"Yes, well, we were going to ask your agency to consider doing a pro bono website for the celebration. It's just a small, one-page website to help us spread the word and get sponsors," he said.

"So," I said, not being able to make eye contact with him, "you aren't sharing information with James?"

"Will, do you really have to ask me that? What would make you question our relationship? No, I'm not sharing information with James, and no, I have no stake in whether your company sells or not," he said, clearly hurt.

My head was swimming. Everything he said made sense, and I felt like an absolute fool.

"Charles, I'm so sorry I doubted you. I just feel so," I said, finally looking him in the eyes, "overwhelmed and…alone. With Paul not wanting to help me with this, the board considering selling the business without my consent, and knowing somehow the acquiring company was getting intel about my efforts, I just felt like everything, and everyone, is pitted against me. I guess the pressure of trying to get the company back on track just became too much and I went against my better judgment."

Charles leaned forward and put his hand on my shoulder. "Will, it's okay. I've been there. Believe me, I've been there. Let's just agree to one thing going forward. If a problem starts to bubble up between us, we'll quickly bring it up and discuss it so that we can get on the same page. I hate that for a few months you thought I was working against you. That's the last thing you needed to have on your plate."

"Thank you, and it's a deal," I said, the relief washing over me. "I need to work on having tough conversations as soon as they're needed."

"We used to have an expression at the last company I ran. 'Have small conversations now to avoid big conversations later.' It means, when a problem starts to arise, immediately bring it out into the open and have dialogue around it, otherwise, the problem or issue will grow and you'll end up having a tougher conversation later," he said.

"Now," he said, standing up and walking over to the whiteboard again, "tell me what you've been up to over here."

"Actually, if you don't mind, I'd love to see if Rachel can join us to help me explain it all, but we also need to do some brainstorming on ways to bring this to life and could use your help," I said.

He agreed and I sent Rachel a text asking if she could join. Two minutes later she arrived at my office.

CHAPTER 28

"So, where do you think you need the most help with ideas?" Charles asked. We had spent the last 45 minutes walking Charles through our structure for building an Undeniable Culture. Surprisingly, he had suggested zero changes and complimented us on how thorough the thinking was.

Undeniable Culture

Step 1: Authentic Foundation

1. Purpose, Vision, Tenets, and Values (PVTV)

2. Core Identity

3. Doing Good Together

Step 2: Trusting Team

1. Focused Leader

2. United Leadership Team

3. Active Meetings

Step 3: Inclusive Environment

1. Live the Values

2. Open Communication

3. Genuine Relationships

"Let's see… with building an Authentic Foundation, we feel really good about our PVTV and Doing Good Together. Less so on finding our Core Identity," Rachel said. She highlighted *PVTV* and *Doing Good Together* in green. "For building a Trusting Team, I think we finally have our Focused Leader—I'm joking Will… kinda. I think we need more work on having a United Leadership Team and creating Active Meetings…"

"We can work on those in our Leadership Team meeting tomorrow," I said, breaking in.

"Perfect," she said, highlighting Focused Leader in green. "Let's look at building an Inclusive Environment. I think we're doing a good job with Live the Values, especially with the addition of adding Acknowledgments to our company meetings, but Open Communication is still something we need to work on. In terms of Genuine Relationships…what do you think of that one, Will?"

I thought for a minute and said, "I think we're on the right path, but that one, like most of these, will take time."

"It's interesting," Charles said, "that you have Genuine Relationships last in the list. It almost seems like the other eight components add up to creating Genuine Relationships."

"How so?" I asked.

"If you're doing good together, like the event you just told me about, you're giving people a chance to form new kinds of bonds with each other. And by acknowledging each other, people will have more affection and appreciation for one another," he said.

"And by having more Active Meetings, where people have enough trust with each other to speak openly, they're more likely to form tighter relationships!" Rachel said.

"Exactly," Charles said. "So that one might not be a problem area, per se, but is rather something that will come over time if you're focusing on the other eight."

"Makes sense," Rachel said. "So we have a little under two months to make significant progress on these items."

We all looked back at the whiteboard, which now clearly showed the areas we needed to focus on.

Undeniable Culture

Step 1: Authentic Foundation

1. Purpose, Vision, Tenets, and Values (PVTV)

2. Core Identity

3. Doing Good Together

Step 2: Trusting Team

1. Focused Leader

2. United Leadership Team

3. Active Meetings

Step 3: Inclusive Environment

1. Live the Values

2. Open Communication

3. Genuine Relationships

"Core Identity is one that I still need to think about. It's not something we can start acting on until I figure out what we stand for. So let's put a pin in that one," I said.

Rachel nodded and said, "So let's talk about ways we can make progress against having a United Leadership Team, Active Meetings, and Open Communication." She turned the whiteboard around to the other side and began writing.

United Leadership Team	Active Meetings	Open Communication
1.	1.	1.
2.	2.	2.
3.	3.	3.

"You guys sure like having things grouped in threes, don't you?" Charles asked.

Rachel pointed at me and said, "Don't look at me, he's the one who has a thing about threes."

Laughing, I said, "What's not to like about threes? There were three stooges, three musketeers, and lest we forget that the Chicago Bulls had not one, but TWO three-peats!"

"Okay, okay, we get it," Rachel said. "Let's get to work on finding ways to bring these three components to life. Who wants to start?"

"I'll just say one thing first," Charles said. "So far what we have listed is fairly universal for any company. I can look at this model and apply it to all of the businesses I've run in the past. In fact, I wish I could go back and do just that! As we move into talking about actionable ways to bring these elements to life, you two should be comfortable being very specific about what your business needs to do."

"Makes sense. I have an idea. How about we each grab a stack of these sticky notes and brainstorm for five minutes on our own, then we can see what we came up with and plot them under the right area?" I suggested.

They both agreed, and five minutes later we had several dozen sticky notes. Rachel collected them and began working to put them on the whiteboard.

While she was doing that, Charles and I sat on the couch. "So," Charles said, "now that you can rule me out as someone involved in trying to steal your company, who is on your list of current suspects?"

"Well, I've ruled out Codeword 9, Massive, and Brainstick, and yes, you," I said, smiling at him. "So at this point I honestly have no suspects. Since the board told me it's a private equity firm, I have no idea who could possibly be behind it."

Charles said, "You might have to look a little deeper on this, Will. Just keep your eyes open and keep doing the work you're doing. I think...,"

"Okay, all done!" Rachel said. We both turned and looked at the whiteboard.

United Leadership Team	Active Meetings	Open Communication
1. Honest dialogue	1. Pre-reads	1. Share (some) finances
2. Time outside of office	2. Focused agenda	2. Overcommunicate
3. Greater transparency	3. Active meeting leader	3. Open up the office

Rachel spent the next few minutes walking us through how each of the items came together. In most cases, there were several sticky notes that spoke to each of them. We debated a few, but overall we were on the same page.

The biggest discussion was around, "Open up the office."

"Just so I understand what you're saying," Charles said, "you want to take down the cubicles and put in desks, and you want no one to have a personal office any more? Are you sure you want to give this up?" He looked around the room, making sure I realized what I was saying.

"I've had a personal office since it was possible, but honestly, I think it would be very freeing to give it up. I have to think about it, but yes, it's probably the right thing to do. The team has to see that I'm willing to sacrifice just as much as anyone else is asked to."

"I like it, and I'm willing to give up my office as well," Rachel said. "What I like most about this list is that I can see how we can start working on these items immediately."

"Agreed. In fact, I'll be able to use a lot of this in tomorrow's leadership meeting," I said.

"I want to point something out to both of you," Charles said. "This is a great list, and working on implementing these things will absolutely help you build an Undeniable Culture. But you should know that the work you've been doing so far is already having an effect. I know it only feels like a few changes, but I can tell those changes are making an impact. First of all, Will, you have a renewed sense of energy for making this company great, which is terrific to see, and what's required to make this kind of turnaround."

"Thanks for saying that," I said. "I can feel it, too."

"And I can tell a difference in you, if I'm being honest," Rachel said.

"And second of all," Charles continued, "I could tell things had changed just by walking through the office with Tina earlier. It feels different. I'm not sure I could point to any one thing, but from when I was here last until today, there's definitely a higher energy level going on. It's starting to feel like it did in the early days."

"That is very encouraging," I said. "It's funny, I was thinking the opposite about our office environment given how charged up and excited everyone was just a week ago. But I know these things take time and yes, we're probably already in a better spot than when we started this process. That said, we've got a lot of work to do!"

"And I," Charles said, "have a lot of riding left to do. I'm going to hit the road. It was great seeing you both, and Will, I look forward to our next meeting."

Charles exited, and Rachel began copying down the notes from the whiteboard. I did the same and we both snapped a photo of the board.

As she packed up her things, she said, “This is great work we did today, Will. There’s only one thing really missing.”

“What’s that?” I asked.

“Paul,” she said.

CHAPTER 29

The leadership meeting was about to start, and I still hadn't been able to grab Paul and get on the same page with him. After the meeting with Charles and Rachel, we texted back and forth about trying to find time, but our schedules didn't match up. I had hoped to catch him before the meeting for at least a few minutes, but I hadn't seen him yet this morning.

Almost as if on cue, the clock turned to 9 a.m., the start time of the meeting, and Paul entered. As he made his way to his seat, I said, "Okay team, as I mentioned previously, we're going to start each of our leadership team meetings with one of us reciting our PVTV. I can do it again—Lord knows I've practiced it enough—but I'd love it if someone else wanted to step up."

Although I had very little expectations that he might have memorized the PVTV by now, I looked at Paul to see if he might raise his hand. Instead, he looked down, avoiding eye contact. So be it. Rachel began to raise her hand when Ahmet said, "I'll do it! I've been working on it during all my drive-time to and from the office this week and I think I'm ready."

"Great, go for it, Ahmet," I said, truly excited that someone other than Rachel had stepped up.

He got through it with only a few mistakes and we all cheered when he was done.

"That was terrific. I hope the rest of you are preparing because we're all going to have to learn it. As a reminder, the reason we do that is to stay focused on why we're here. It helps us frame our decisions and steer the ship if we get off course.

"Now, today we're going to do something a little different," I said, looking around at each of them. "I haven't been completely honest about what's going on, and it's time I changed that. You all deserve to be told the truth, always."

Paul said, "Will, what are you…"

"It's okay, Paul," I said, cutting him off. "I've thought this through and not only is it the right thing to do, but it's also the only way to give us a chance."

I then spent the next 15 minutes telling the leadership team everything that had been going on. The possible sale, the meetings with the other agencies, and the work we'd been doing on building an Undeniable Culture.

When I finished, everyone looked a little stunned. Paul exhaled audibly and gave me a look that seemed to scream, "seriously?" But I knew this was the right move.

"So, let's start with questions, because I know you must have a lot, and then we'll start diving into rebuilding this company together," I said.

Steve said, "Why didn't you tell us sooner?"

"Because we aren't supposed to tell anyone," Paul said, glaring at me. "The group that wants to buy us made that explicitly clear. And when you're potentially going to be acquired, you don't want to let any leaks happen because that could jeopardize our ability to hire new team members or win new accounts. Imagine, Steve, if RedBrick found out right now that we might be bought. They'd immediately sign with Massive and be done with this RFP process."

"That's definitely correct," Steve said. "So I guess we all need to keep this to ourselves, huh?"

"Yes," I said, "Paul's right about the seriousness of this and we do need to keep it quiet. And I wouldn't have told you all about this if I didn't trust each and every one of you."

Martha said, "So we have about a month and a half before the board makes a decision, is that what you said?"

I nodded.

No one else spoke up, so Rachel said, "Okay, well I'm all-in on trying to turn this company around in order to sway the board's decision. I say we get started on your plan, Will. Everyone agree?"

Everyone nodded their head in agreement.

"Will, want me to share the plan as it is right now with everyone?" she asked.

"Go for it," I said. She walked up to the whiteboard and wrote:

Undeniable Culture

Step 1: Authentic Foundation

1. Purpose, Vision, Tenets, and Values (PVTV)

2. Core Identity

3. Doing Good Together

Step 2: Trusting Team

1. Focused Leader

2. United Leadership Team

A. Honest Dialogue

B. Time Outside of Office

C. Greater Transparency

3. Active Meetings

A. Pre-reads

B. Focused Agenda

C. Active Meeting Leader

Step 3: Inclusive Environment

1. Live the Values

2. Open Communication

A. Share (some) finances

B. Overcommunicate

C. Open up the Office

3. Genuine Relationships

I stood up and talked them through how we had made it to this point, emphasizing that the three areas with sub-bullets—United Leadership Team, Active Meetings, and Open Communication—were the areas we had identified as having the most opportunity to make improvements over the next six weeks.

"So, I guess you telling us all of this is part of the Honest Dialogue bullet?" Martha said.

I laughed and said, "Yes, I suppose it is. Mostly what that means is that we have to be honest with each other, especially within this team. And that is only possible if we trust each other and know we have each other's backs."

I thought about what Sarah had told me about the team possibly not being as open with me about things because I'm the boss, for fear that I might not react the way they hoped.

"And that starts with me being willing to hear bad news. I'm sure there are times in the past that I've reacted negatively to criticism or ideas that go in a different direction than I thought they should, and I will work on that going forward. If you can't feel free to speak your mind in front of me, then we'll never have Honest Dialogue in these meetings."

We spent the next half-hour talking through each of the items. The group had great ideas—other than Paul, who sat silently and checked his phone a lot. That is, until the concept of opening up the office came up.

Ahmet said, "I'm really excited about the Open Communication aspect of this. Do you guys remember the vending problem we had last year?"

"Oh, wow, that's a great call," Martha said.

Rachel said, "I'm not sure I remember what you're talking about. The vending story?"

"That's right, you were on your three-week trip in Europe when this went down," I said. "Ahmet, tell the story."

"Well, you know how our office is kind of split up into areas, with most of the team in The Farm, and several groups in pockets throughout the office? So, one of those groups was tired of walking all the way across the office to the kitchen area to use the vending machine, plus they didn't like all of the selections," he said.

"They didn't like that super long, 45-second walk to the kitchen? Let me guess, was it Travis's team?" Rachel said.

Ahmet laughed and said, "Well, I'm not going to name names, but yes, it was Travis's team. To be fair, they also felt like they could save money buying the sodas themselves. So anyway, they asked if they could get a small fridge in their area that they could stock on their own..."

"Sounds reasonable," Rachel said.

"That's what we thought. So of course we said yes, that would be fine. A week went by and the vending guy came by and...well, Paul, you should tell this part," Ahmet said.

"Yeah, so Larry knocks on my office door one day and tells me that something has happened to the amount of product sold in the machine and if it doesn't improve he's going to have to take the machine away. You all might remember when his vending company agreed to put the machine in, they did a headcount of our staff to ensure that enough product would sell to make it worth servicing a machine here. I told him I was surprised, but then he mentioned that he saw a mini-fridge in one of the areas he walked by…"

"Oooohhh," Rachel said, "so Travis's team was not buying products anymore from the machine, and they're like, what, 20% of our workforce…"

"Exactly," Ahmet said. "So Paul brings it up to Will, and they agree that the mini-fridge has to go because we can't have 80% of our company lose out on drinks because one team wants their own mini-fridge."

Steve jumped in. "So Will and Paul tell me I needed to inform Travis that he can't have the mini-fridge anymore. Now, I didn't know any of this about the vending, and I don't know why I didn't ask them what the reasoning was—I assumed it was because it looked junky to have one in the office. I went and told Travis he needed to remove it. And let me just say, he was not happy about that, especially when I told him that it looked too junky in the office."

"So then what happened?" Rachel asked.

"Basically, Travis's entire team developed an attitude, especially toward Will," Martha said. "They basically thought we were being too 'big brother' and 'corporate' on them—these are things I actually heard them say—and one team member even left!"

"All of this happened while I was out for three weeks?" Rachel asked.

"Yep," I said. "It was all very strange to me until I figured out what was going on. I swear I was getting cold stares from Travis's team and I didn't know why. So finally, I pulled Travis into my office and asked him what was going on. I figured he would be honest since he'd been with us from the early days.

"And I'll never forget our conversation. He told me they were upset about us making them remove the mini-fridge. I asked him if he had a better idea, given the vending machine would have to go. That's when I realized he had no idea what I was talking about. Once I explained the situation, he understood my motivation in making the change. After about five minutes, not only was he no longer upset with me, we had come up with a solution. His team would get to decide two of the products in the machine, and we decided to make the price lower in order to match the cost he was paying when he bought in bulk, with the company covering the difference," I said.

"Wow, so all of that, including a team member leaving, could have been solved with just a tiny bit more communication at the beginning?" Rachel said.

"That's right. What a huge lesson that was. Thanks for bringing that up, Ahmet," I said.

"What does 'Open up the office' mean?" Steve asked.

"Ah, yes, well this is bound to be the most controversial. Here's the deal. In my tour of Brainstick, I was able to see an extreme version of what a closed-off office looks like. And let me tell you, it's not good. And I started thinking about how I was unaware of our culture starting to take a hit, mostly because I'm in a personal office and have the door closed too often. Plus, the cubicles we have are too high and restrict people from really engaging.

"What I want us to do is remove those cubes and get everyone desks, and," I said, looking around at each of them, "I want all of us to move out of our offices and into the main area. No one should have their own personal office. It sets the wrong message and disconnects our leaders from the rest of the team."

Paul, unable to take any more of this, said, "Are you kidding? I'm not giving up my office, Will. I have too many important meetings that I can't have out in the open, and you know that."

"I've thought about that," I said, disregarding the contempt in his voice. "And for those that need it, we can change your office into a conference room that essentially is yours to book. When you need to have a closed-door meeting, that room should be available to you. But I'd like everyone to have their main working desk outside of their personal office. And that starts with me. You all can take your time with it, but I'll be moving out this afternoon."

I knew that it was important for everyone to see that I was willing to sacrifice first. I learned this lesson from my coach when I was a college tennis player. It was an incredibly cold afternoon—close to 30 degrees—and extremely windy. Playing tennis in weather like that is near impossible. And yet, Coach had us out there nonetheless.

As he fed us balls, we began to complain. Loudly. After about 15 minutes of this, Coach stopped feeding balls, put his racket down, and took off his gloves, jacket, and beanie. He tossed them to the side, picked his racket back up, and began feeding us balls again.

Stunned that he would be taking clothes *off* in this weather, we were quiet for a few minutes, but it didn't take long before we were complaining again.

"This is ridiculous, we shouldn't be out here!"

"I can't feel my hands, this sucks!"

On and on we complained, and after another 15 minutes went by, Coach stopped feeding balls again, set his racket down, and this time took off his sweatpants, sweatshirt, and the shirt underneath. Now he was standing in his tiny, white shorts, socks, shoes… and nothing else. He picked up his racket and once again began feeding us balls.

It took about 30 seconds before his upper body was bright red from the cold. But he never acted like it bothered him. He just kept going about his business feeding us balls.

I looked at all the gear I had on—two shirts, sweatshirt, sweat pants, beanie—and thought, "Jeez, I'm 20 years old and completely bundled up, and he's in his late 50s and almost naked out here." I noticed the other guys were thinking the same thing, and for the rest of the practice we didn't complain again. Not once.

That day, Coach showed us that he was willing to suffer alongside us, and it was a leadership lesson I never forgot.

Rachel and Ahmet were quickly on board with us removing personal offices, while Martha and Steve had some reservations. And Paul remained obstinate to the entire idea.

"Oh, and one last thing, we're not going to apply for the Best Places to Work award anymore," I said. "We're not going to let some organization that is motivated mostly by earning revenue through submission fees and ticket sales decide what our culture should be. We need to get focused on building an Undeniable Culture, and we need to do it our way."

I could tell Martha wasn't sure about that decision, so I nudged her a little. "Martha, I can tell you have some thoughts about this. Remember, part of our new model is to feel free to speak up and challenge anyone's ideas, especially mine. I would be surprised if you didn't have something to say about this one, given your role over human resources and hiring."

"Well," she said, a bit nervously, "it's just that the Best Places to Work award has been a nice recruiting tool for us. I use it in every interview I do."

"It also helps with our sales opportunities," Ahmet said.

I nodded and said, "I get all of that, and a decision isn't a tough one if there aren't any trade-offs. But I'm certain that when we build a culture that truly brings our team together, where everyone is on the same page and genuinely supports each other, the benefits of that will outweigh the benefits of winning the award."

They seemed to buy that, or at least were willing to see how it would play out.

I looked at my watch and said, "Okay, time is up. Please keep thinking about this model for creating an Undeniable Culture, and share anything you think of. The mission for the next six weeks is to work hard on implementing these changes so we can hopefully see real change before the next board meeting."

As team members started to stand up, Steve said, "I just have to say that I think this was the best Leadership Team meeting we've ever had. Sure, Will, you shared some crazy ideas and I'm not 100% in alignment on dropping the Best Places to Work Award, or moving out of my office, for that matter, but I feel like we finally started listening to each other and working *on the business* rather than *in the business*. I'm pumped about this change!"

Everyone agreed. Well, not everyone. Paul was already out of the room, having quickly made his exit. As good as I felt about the progress thus far, and my job leading us through it, I felt like I was failing miserably at my partnership with Paul.

If I was going to be successful at this, I'd need to figure out how to solve that piece of the puzzle. And fast.

CHAPTER 30

Later that afternoon, I received a text from Steve that said:

Are you in your office?

I quickly replied:

Sure am, what's up?

He sent back:

Be right there, don't go anywhere.

30 seconds later Steve bounded into my office. Slightly out of breath, he said, "Will, we just got the response from RedBrick..."

"Did we win?!" I asked, interrupting him.

"Unfortunately, we didn't win," he said. "But...

"So....we lost? I can't believe it," I said, immediately going through the ramifications of losing RedBrick. Not only would a huge piece of our revenue go away from losing their account, but the board would almost definitely agree to sell the business because there's nothing that shows your business is struggling more than losing your biggest account.

And we'd have to lay people off, which we'd never had to do in the past. What would that be, 15 people? No, probably more like

20. My stomach started to drop when Steve said, "No, we didn't lose either."

"What do you mean?" I asked.

"Well, apparently they couldn't decide between our two shops. Half the team liked Massive, and half the team liked us. And before you ask, I couldn't get an answer on who Mark liked the best," he said.

Dumbfounded, I said, "So what does that mean? They're going to keep the account as is, with our agencies continuing to do the work we've been doing?"

"Nope, they're going to have final, in-person pitches to decide the winner. We're still in this!" he nearly shouted.

"Well, that's certainly good news. Not exactly what I was hoping for, but definitely better than losing the account. Okay, I assume you're going to get the team together and start formulating a plan. You should include Ahmet, obviously, as he oversees our new business pitches and has the latest creative," I said.

"Definitely. This will be an all-hands attack. I'm so pumped," he said. Then he got a confused look on his face and said, "Wait, I thought you were supposed to be out of your office by now?"

"I still have a few more hours. Don't worry, you'll see me out in the main area by end of day," I said. The truth was, I had been procrastinating. I didn't want to give up my office, even though I knew it was the right decision, and something I would have to do first to show everyone that I was as committed as I was asking them to be.

He smiled and said, "Well, count on me to be the next one to do it after you. Okay, I gotta go start getting the team together to prep for the pitch…"

"Wait a second, when is the pitch?" I asked.

"Let me see," he said, looking at his phone. "Says here it's June 14th. See ya."

Steve left the office and I thought about that for a minute. June 14th, why did that date seem peculiar…

Oh, jeez. That's the day before the final board meeting!

CHAPTER 31

I found a few empty cardboard boxes in the storage area behind the kitchen, brought them to my office, and started packing up my stuff. As I'd always been a bit of a minimalist when it came to "stuff" in my office, there actually wasn't a lot to pack and I only used one of the boxes.

After packing, I swung by Paul's office and knocked.

"Come on in," I heard him say through the door.

I opened the door and poked my head in, "Hey, any chance you can help me with something for a minute?"

He looked up and made a face that was a mix between confusion and annoyance. "Uh, sure, what do you need?" he asked.

"I just need you to help me move something real quick," I said. "Follow me."

There was an area of our office that we hadn't yet needed to move into. It was on the opposite side of the floor from my personal office, and in it we stored a bunch of our extra furniture. I led Paul to that room and pointed at a desk.

"That's my new desk, and I need help moving it over to the area outside my office," I said.

"Are you serious?" Paul said. He looked back toward where we came from and said, "Don't we have people who can help with this kind of thing?"

"Nope, turns out we didn't hire any furniture movers as permanent staff. I checked. So it's you and me, buddy," I said.

"Okay, well you're getting the heavy end," he said.

We lifted up the desk and immediately ran into a problem. The desk would only fit vertically through the doorway, so we had to lift it up in an awkward manner. After we made it halfway through, we had to pivot the desk 90 degrees to make it.

After that, we started making our way through the office. We were met with quite a few curious stares from team members.

"Remind you of anything?" I asked, grunting.

A smile appeared on Paul's face. "Yes, this reminds me of the very first office we had, down on Zonolite. Of course, this is nothing compared to that. I think we worked for three straight days, painting, moving furniture, running cables…we even built a doorway, remember that?"

"We sure did. I kind of miss those days," I said.

"I know what you mean. Things were so much simpler back then. And we were always," he said, looking up at me, "on the same page, weren't we?"

I nodded and said, "That we were. I'd like to try to get back to that if we could."

We made it to my office and I pointed to where I wanted the desk to be. I had decided to keep my desk close to the office and then turn my office into a conference room that I could use for group meetings or one-on-one meetings, only closing the door when it was absolutely necessary.

"Need any help with anything else?" he asked.

"No, I think I've got it from here. Thanks for the help," I said.

"You got it," Paul said, and headed back to his office. Part of me was hoping that doing this together would get us talking a little and remind Paul of the old days. That seemed to work and it felt good to have at least a little bit of an uncontested conversation with him. Another part of me had hoped he would say, *now let's go get a desk for me so I can join you out here*. While that didn't happen, I decided to take the win.

I walked into my office and put the filing cabinet on top of my chair, and rolled it out to the new desk. After I set everything up, I took a seat and looked around. I could see a few people looking my way wondering what I was doing, but they quickly looked away when I saw them. Mostly, I just saw what looked like a small city of high-walled cubicles, so I couldn't see many people directly. That would change soon enough. I hoped this part of the strategy—opening up the office more to allow the team to form deeper bonds, creating serendipitous interactions, and ultimately creating more trust amongst the team—would work the way I planned. Oh well, we had to start somewhere. "Begin the begin," as Charles had said.

I opened up my laptop, threw my headphones on, and started knocking out email.

CHAPTER 32

A few days later, everyone had once again gathered together in The Farm for the company meeting. I could certainly feel a new buzz of energy in the room as I tried to quiet them down.

"Okay, everyone, it's time to get started with the company meeting," I said. Once everyone quieted down, I said. "Now, I know that when you all came in yesterday you noticed something different about your workstations."

"You took out all of the cubes!" Someone shouted from the back.

Over the weekend we hired a company to remove the old, high-walled cubes and in their place install desks for each team member.

Laughing, I said, "That's right, we did. I think you'll admit, at a minimum it makes it a lot easier to have these company meetings. I can actually see all of you this time!

"But I'm curious if anyone else wants to weigh in on why the leadership team and I decided to do this. And," I said, patting my desk which was right next to me, "why I'm now sitting out in the open instead of in my office."

The room was quiet for a minute before a young woman in the front row raised her hand.

"Yes, Charlotte, why do you think we did this?" I said.

"I guess, well, maybe you did it because you wanted things more... open, I guess?" she said.

"That's right! And why do you think we'd want things to be more open?"

Starting to gain more courage, she said, "Well, I think it's probably because we are a creative agency and the more we work together, the more creative we'll be?"

"That's a great answer. The more we collaborate and bring ideas from anywhere in the company, the more creative we'll be," I said. "Great job, Charlotte. Does anyone else have an idea of why we might be doing this?"

Rachel, seeing that no more hands were going to go up, raised her hand. I called on her and she said, "I know one of the reasons we talked about this was because we want to have less barriers, figuratively and literally, that keep us from feeling like a team. The more we wall each other off, the more divided we will be. And, I'm sure some of you noticed that I also moved out of my personal office. That's because I want to make sure I'm more connected to everyone and that you know you can approach me anytime you want. The goal is to make sure we're coming together and working more like a team."

"Exactly, thanks, Rach," I said. Then I looked at the group and said, "You might recall that I kicked off our last meeting reciting our PVTV, minus any unicorns I might add. And I promised that this time, one of our leadership team members would give it a try. So...who's up for it?"

I looked around at the various leadership team members, each scattered throughout the room.

Several hands went up.

"Martha," I said, "why don't you give it a go?"

Martha stood up and said, "Okay, here goes...Our Purpose is to Inspire Happiness through positive relationships....impactful work...and..."

"Doing good!" someone shouted from the back.

"Yes, and doing good! Thanks for the help," Martha said, smiling. She took a deep breath and said, "And our Vision is to be the world's best...no, sought after by the world's best companies... for our creative problem solving!"

Everyone cheered, seeing that she was working hard to get it right.

"We will do this by attracting and retaining exceptional people, building...oh, what's the word?" she said. Then she looked at everyone and said, "That wasn't rhetorical, seriously, what's the word?"

"Remarkable!" another person shouted.

Laughing, Martha said, "Right, thanks, Todd. Building remarkable products and experiences...and striving for operational excellence!"

Another round of cheers, this time with a few whoops and a couple hollers.

"And now for our Values," she said. "We believe in putting the team first, thinking positively, celebrating diversity…doing good, and having fun!"

The room erupted and the people around her gave her high fives.

"Excellent job, Martha! And at our next company meeting, I want someone that's not on the leadership team to be brave enough to attempt our PVTV. And, just to give you a little incentive, whoever gives it a go will get a company-branded, one-of-a-kind Patagonia pullover," I said.

Once again, everyone cheered. It felt really great to start a meeting with this kind of excitement.

"Okay, Paul and Rachel, are you ready to walk us through the rest of the agenda?" I asked.

They both got up and made their way to the front. Rachel said, "Can we give Martha another round of applause for doing our PVTV?"

Another boisterous round of clapping and hooting followed, and Rachel said, "Now, I hope you all are starting to remember parts of our PVTV, and eventually you'll be ready to say it by heart, but does anyone remember what the three pillars of our Tenets are? And remember, our Tenets are the things we will focus on in order to achieve our Vision."

A team member raised her hand and said, "I don't know them exactly, but one is focused on having great people. The second, I think, is focused on making sure our work is excellent, and the third is operational excellence, I remember that one."

"Yes, Kelly, I would expect you to remember that one since you're on the operations team," Rachel said, smiling. "And you got the gist of them correct. From now on, we're going to run our company meetings against our Tenets, because those are the things we need to focus on in order to be successful."

Paul turned on the large monitor on the wall and the opening slide popped up:

Company Meeting Agenda

1. ***Attract and Retain Exceptional People***
2. ***Build Remarkable Products and Experiences***
3. ***Strive for Operational Excellence***
4. ***Acknowledgments***
5. ***Questions (and hopefully, Answers)***

Paul said, "Martha, looks like you're up." Martha, as head of Human Resources, came up to the front and began giving her update on "Attract and Retain Exceptional People."

When she was done, she handed it over to Steve and Ahmet, who talked about the work we're doing for clients and new prospects (Build Remarkable Products and Experiences). The majority of their section was focused on the RedBrick pitch.

"As I'm sure you are all aware by now, next month we have the big RedBrick presentation. It's an in-person meeting, and it's us against one other agency for all the marbles. It's going to take all of us to make sure this is the best presentation we've ever done, so I hope you're ready to do a little brainstorming right now," Steve said.

I wasn't sure what he had in mind with the brainstorming activity as we weren't ready to dig into the creative idea for the pitch just yet, but I did know that Steve had requested 20 minutes for his section.

Ahmet said, "One of the things we want your help with is how we can show RedBrick what we stand for. As a leadership team, we're calling that our Core Identity. What is it that we all, as a company, believe to be our greatest strength?"

While Ahmet was talking, Steve brought a large, rolling whiteboard out to the front of the room.

"Don't be shy," Ahmet said. "We really want any and all ideas at this point. Just shout out what you're thinking and Steve will write it on the whiteboard."

For the next 15 minutes, someone would call out what they thought might be our Core Identity, the group would discuss it, and then if it warranted making the whiteboard, Steve would write it on a Post-It note and stick it on the board. When they were finished, he grouped the notes into four possible directions.

Possible Core Identities

CREATIVITY **USER EXPERIENCE** **AGILITY** **HEART**

They thanked everyone and shared next steps for the RedBrick pitch, and then passed the stage over to Paul and Rachel who would take the team through, "Striving for Operational Excellence." As they went through the numbers with everyone, sharing more than we had before so that people had a better idea of how our business worked, I began to think about the four areas that had been identified.

Creativity was interesting, and certainly made sense for a marketing agency like ours. The problem was that it didn't really work for the entire company. For example, while the project managers understood the importance of creativity, they surely wouldn't say that's what they believe is the core of what we stand for, because they don't impact creativity at all.

I found the concept of User Experience intriguing. Using the project manager example, I could see that even they could act on the idea of making sure the user experience was great, as they work directly with our clients and could focus on making their experience terrific. However, when it was discussed amongst the group, there didn't seem to be much passion for it. I got the feeling that it made good sense, but wasn't an area where people really believed we shined.

Agility was very interesting, and not something I would have thought to consider. Everyone seemed to agree that we typically competed against larger shops—Massive was much larger than us, for example—and we could use our size and entrepreneurial instincts to move more quickly. The problem, as someone pointed out, was that we likely wouldn't always be small. And while we could always try to make sure we were entrepreneurial, if we hired someone into our company when we were a 250-person agency and told them that our unique attribute was that we were incredibly agile, they likely would have a hard time believing it, as would clients.

Heart…now that was interesting. I wonder…

"Okay, Will, are you ready to come up and take us through Acknowledgments?" I heard Rachel say.

"Absolutely! Acknowledgments have become my favorite part of the meeting already, no offense to the riveting presentation you just gave, of course," I said with a smile.

I opened up by first doing my own acknowledgment, this time recognizing Tina for doing such a great job not only making sure that any of our guests felt welcomed and taken care of—which I attributed to our Value, "Thinking Positively,"—but also for always being willing to help anyone with literally anything.

"I once heard you helped a team member who was stressed about her upcoming exam in her MBA class study the night before the test. Now, if that's not Team First, I don't know what is!" I said.

Tina blushed as everyone cheered for her.

"It's true!" shouted Bobbi, who was a part of the Account Services team. "And I aced the test!"

Everyone cheered again, and then Tina raised her hand. I called on her and she said, "I'd like to acknowledge Steve, because every day he comes in, he checks on me and makes sure I'm doing okay. And some of you might have noticed that I have a small cactus on my desk at the front. That's because I told him a week ago that the cactus I'd had for eight years finally died, and the next day he brought me a new one."

Everyone clapped for Steve, and he went next. It went on and on like that, with one person acknowledging someone, and then that person doing the same for someone else. As with the last time, there were some tears, lots of laughs, and a general sense of caring that everyone had for each other.

I began to realize that this innate sense of caring for one another was indeed a special thing for our company. Long ago, Paul and I had decided to make sure that our agency was a place people enjoyed working. We didn't use the word "culture" back then because, quite frankly, we hadn't studied business and leadership when we started the company. However, it was clear even then that we wanted to be a place where people cared for one another. Creating an opportunity for the team to acknowledge one another, while a random idea that hit me at Danielle's school assembly, was exactly what the team needed in order to express that heart.

At that moment it hit me: **Our Core Identity was in fact our Heart!** I would need to think through how to manifest that so it made sense for our team, clients, and potential clients, but it felt right. It aligned with our Purpose of Inspiring Happiness, it was one of the areas that the team had arrived at during the brainstorming exercise with Steve and Ahmet, and it was readily apparent in the way everyone was acknowledging one another.

Realizing that we only had about five minutes left of the meeting, I waited until the current person was finished and said, "That was great, everyone, and I can see there are many of you that want to keep going, but unfortunately we have to move on to the last point of the agenda. Keep in mind, you don't have to wait until our company meeting to recognize your team members!

"For the last part of our meeting, I want to encourage you to ask any question that you might have, the more awkward the better. We want to start making this a more open company, where everyone is able to be heard and spoken to honestly. And remember, there are no dumb questions. If you are wondering about something, there are absolutely other people that are wondering that same thing. So," I said, stretching my arms out, "ask away."

It took a minute but a hand came up from the far right corner of The Farm.

"Susan, thanks for being the first one to ask a question," I said.

"You bet, and I think this is an easy one, but this new layout," she said, motioning to the new cubicle-less Farm, "looks like it will be a disaster when it comes to being able to focus on your work. Personally, I'm having a small anxiety attack just thinking about working in here right now." She laughed a little at that, but I got the gist.

"Yes, that is something we've thought about. You obviously all saw that not only had we moved your equipment from a cubicle to a desk, but we also supplied all of you with company-branded, noise-canceling headphones," I said, grabbing the headphones off my desk. "The rule is simple: if someone has their headphones on, that means they're working and they should not be disturbed. That's where we will start, but I've seen other companies do things like have a flag on their desk and when it's upright, that means,

'Leave me alone, I'm trying to get work done.' So we'll see what works best for us. And, since the leadership team is moving out of our offices, we now have a handful of more conference rooms, so if you need a few hours of quiet time, feel free to book one of those rooms. The last thing we want is to make this a difficult place for you to work."

"Yes, John," I said, seeing his hand pop up. "What would you like to know?"

John stood up and said, "Well, as you know, I've been here for a few years, and the last six months have felt…"

"Go ahead," I said, sensing he was worried about saying something that might offend me, "this is a safe space and I want you to speak honestly."

"Thanks," he said, blushing a little. "I guess it's felt less than awesome, and the first year or so felt really great. And then I see these changes that you're making and it makes me wonder if you're worried about the company. Like, are you thinking we might go out of business or something if we don't make these changes?"

"Now that's a great question," I said. "And you're not wrong. The company has lost its way over the last six months, maybe even a little longer than that. What I believe is happening is that we have lost the focus on our culture. We've let it morph and change into something that is less than awesome, as you said. What we need to do is create an Undeniable Culture, one that is based on our Authentic Foundation—who we really are as a company and what our beliefs are. We do that as a Trusting Team, meaning we are aligned and focused as one entity, and by creating an Inclusive

Environment, one where we create genuine relationships with one another and allow for open dialogue—including questions like the one you just asked."

I paused for a moment and looked around at everyone. While I couldn't tell them about the acquisition process, I wanted to be as upfront as I possibly could.

"I'll be honest with you, I'm worried that we might not have started this process soon enough. Will we go out of business if we don't create an Undeniable Culture? Probably not. There are plenty of agencies that have subpar cultures that are still in existence, some of which are actually growing. I don't know about you, but I don't want to work at a place like that. We have a chance to build something really special, and it's going to take all of us to make that happen. I, and the entire leadership team, want you to be more direct and honest with what you think this business needs, and we're committed to making the changes necessary to ensure we get back on track and truly create a place where we all love coming every day."

Before I could say another word, Tina began clapping. And then another person joined in, and before long the entire company was clapping. As always happens when a large group is clapping together long enough, their applause synced up and they were clapping in unison.

Tears began welling up in my eyes. Not because I had delivered some rousing speech—I hadn't—and not because they were clapping for me—they weren't. By clapping though, they had agreed as a team, without using any words, that they were in this together and were ready to fight the good fight to save this company.

Looking at my watch, I realized we were a minute over time. I put my hands out to indicate for them to stop clapping, and said, "Thank you, everyone, it means a lot to see that you are up for this challenge and ready to create something special, together. It means the world to know that. And, as you'll see, my desk is out in the open so anytime you have an idea or question, please come right over to me."

Everyone began getting up and heading back to their workstations. I caught Rachel's eye and she gave me a big smile and a thumbs up. Several team members shared how much they enjoyed the meeting as they went past, and one of them even high-fived me.

I sat down at my desk and, leaning back, thought about what had just happened. We gave the team a little bit of knowledge about what was happening, and they immediately rallied together to help us solve the problem. Why had I been so reluctant to involve everyone before? Maybe in my mind I thought that, because they aren't shareholders in the company, they wouldn't be interested in digging in and helping us build the company back.

But they showed me today that they did truly care, and why wouldn't they? This was the place they chose to work and would consequently spend over 40 hours a week at. Of course they wanted to believe in the company and play a part of making it stronger. And, until now, I'd never given them the chance to do so.

The question remained: with only a month before the next board meeting, was there enough time to make a difference?

MONTH 6

CHAPTER 33

It was a beautiful Saturday morning and Sarah and I were again at the park with Danielle. And once more, my mind was stuck back at the office.

Sarah and Danielle were holding hands up on the gravel path ahead of me. I was about 10 feet behind, absently kicking pebbles while my mind raced.

The progress we had made since the last company meeting had seemed, to me at least, to be truly transformational. The office felt entirely different than it ever had before. While it was true that a year or two earlier our culture seemed great, I now realize that our fast growth had been masking some pretty major problems. With no defined Values, the lack of an authentic Purpose driving us forward, and hardly any actual effort to ensure our culture was sound, we were simply being swept forward with our momentum. New wins and new team members can make all the problems go away…until the growth stops, which is exactly what had happened to us.

Just then, a pebble hit me right in the middle of the chest. I looked up to see Danielle and Sarah laughing, and they immediately started running off the path into the open field in the middle of the park.

"I thought I told you whippersnappers to leave me alone!" I yelled in my best old man voice. "Now I'm gonna have to teach you a lesson!"

I gave chase and, pretending to labor as I ran, eventually caught them. I gently tackled Danielle and began to tickle her, while Sarah pretended to punch my back. Eventually, they overtook me and pinned me to the ground, and Danielle sat on my stomach.

"I hope you yearned your lesson!" she said.

"And what lesson is that?" I asked.

"To stop being so boring!" she said. Then she high-fived Sarah and jumped off of me.

"Danielle," Sarah said, pointing over to the swingset a little ways away, "why don't you go over and swing for a few minutes while your daddy and I talk?"

"Okay!" Danielle said, and began running toward the swingset.

"I'm sorry," I preemptively said. "I know I'm distracted, and I hate that! Heck, it was my idea to go to the park this morning in the hopes of taking my mind off of everything. But with the RedBrick pitch on Monday and the board meeting on Tuesday, it's just…"

"I know, honey, it's okay. I get the importance of the RedBrick pitch. It means you either double your business with them or it goes away. And then, of course the board meeting is huge, because you'll know their decision on whether or not to sell the company. I've given you a hard time before, but this time I really do get it," she said. "Let's start with the RedBrick pitch, how are you feeling about it?"

I sat up, excited and appreciative to talk it out with her. "Honestly,

I'm feeling great about it. Our ideas are strong, our team is prepared, and we'll do a final prep tomorrow…"

"On Sunday? And when were you going to tell me this?" she asked.

"Uh, now? Sorry, I definitely should have told you. We have to practice the pitch a few more times to make sure we're hitting our marks, and with the pitch being on Monday, that just leaves…"

"Sunday. Okay, I get it. You won't mind if I take Danielle over to my boyfriend's house, right? He has a hot tub and she thinks he's hilarious."

"Ha ha. Very funny. I deserved that," I said, laughing.

"Okay, so you're feeling good about the pitch. Tell me about how the team is doing and what you think will happen at the board meeting. Oh, and did you figure out who was behind the leaks?"

"No, I haven't, but as you know I did figure out it wasn't Charles, which was a huge relief," I said.

"I never thought it was Charles. That just seemed…off. He's always had your back," she said.

"I know. We had a good talk and from now on, when any issue arises, we've agreed to immediately talk it through with each other and get it out in the open. So, no, I have no idea at this point who has been behind the leaks. But either way, it doesn't quite matter as much since it's not another agency that wants to buy us, but a private equity firm. They likely want to buy us and then, over the next five to seven years, buy other companies to merge with ours and eventually sell the entire thing to someone else," I said.

"Sounds like fun," she said with more than a hint of sarcasm in her voice.

"Well, I don't think it will matter for me whether or not it's fun. They clearly aren't considering keeping me on board, otherwise I would have been part of the process. But, there's nothing I can do about that other than hope with the board meeting on Tuesday that the progress we've made has been enough."

Sarah, keeping her eye on Danielle, who was chatting it up with another girl her age on the swings, said, "And how is it not having a personal office and working out in the open with everyone?"

"I love it! I can't believe I was ever foolish enough to lock myself up in an office. I was missing so much. And several people have come up to me to ask a question when I know they wouldn't have before. It's also been fun to watch the other leaders move out of their offices. They've all told me how much more they enjoy being out with everyone. Well, all but one..."

"Let me guess," she said, turning to me, "Paul doesn't like it."

"Worse," I said. "He's the only one that has yet to move out of his office. I asked him about it on Friday and he said he's just been busy, what with the upcoming pitching and board meeting, and that he'd get to it eventually."

"I'm sorry you two haven't been able to get on the same page with all of this," she said.

I nodded and said, "I can't help but feel that's on me. Paul means well and I'm throwing a huge wrench in all of our plans, so I probably should have been more sympathetic to his concerns. Just another thing to learn for next time," I said.

"Well, come Tuesday night, we'll either be celebrating the sale of your company, or…not the sale of your company. Let's order in," she said.

"Sounds great," I said. We got up and began walking over to the swingset. She reached out and took my hand in hers, and for a few minutes, everything felt right in the world.

CHAPTER 34

The RedBrick office was just up the interstate in an area of town referred to as Blueberry Hills. I had never quite understood why this area was called that, as it was completely flat and I'd never seen a fruit of any kind there.

Their office was, as one might imagine, made of red brick and rose 25 floors. We parked in one of the visitor parking spots and made our way to the receptionist.

Steve led the way, with a senior account manager, our head of media planning, two creatives, and me. One by one we signed in, showed our ID, and received a visitor badge. We made our way over to a table in the waiting area to wait for our host to come and get us.

"So, you're sure about this approach?" Steve said, looking at me and asking the question he'd asked several times already on the drive over.

I smiled at him and said, "Yes, I'm sure. First of all, Mark wanted to hear what we stand for. He made that clear to me when we met. Plus, I'm ready for us to be more bold about who we are and what we believe.

"And don't worry," I said, looking at the rest of our team, "what you all have put together—our creative idea, our strategy to bring it to life through media, and how we'll manage their account effectively and hit their goals—is brilliant. I'd hire us just on that if I could. But we need to also give them a glimpse of who we are deep down."

"Looks like it's go-time," Steve said, standing up. "Hi, Carrie!"

The young woman approached our group, shook Steve's hand, and said to the rest of us, "Okay, if you all are ready, I'll take you up to the top floor for the pitch."

"Lead the way!" Steve said, and we followed Carrie through the security doors—she had to scan us through one by one—and to the elevator bank. We entered and after scanning her badge once again, hit the button for the 25th floor.

"So, I understand you had Massive in earlier today. Any chance you'll tell us how that went?" I asked, always trying to get an edge when possible.

"That's right, they came in at 10 this morning. There were a whole bunch of them, actually. Probably double the size of your team," she said. "As far as how it went, I wasn't in the room, so you won't get any scoop out of me."

The elevator reached the top floor and we all got off. Carrie led us past the receptionist desk and said, "This is the executive floor. The entire C-suite has their offices up here. And here we are, the executive conference room."

She opened the doors to a fairly large conference room with giant windows along one side. Steve asked Carrie some logistical questions—how to connect to the projector, if there was an audio hook-up, etc.—and I walked over to check out the view. It was spectacular and, like our office, had a great view of Foothills Park.

"So, let's see," Carrie said, looking at her watch. "You have about five minutes before our team arrives. Can I get you anything else?"

"No, thanks, I think we're good," Steve said. "Any last-minute advice?"

She laughed and said, "I don't think so. Just be yourselves and I'm sure you'll do fine." With that, she left us alone in the room.

We took the seats closest to the projector, leaving the seats at the far end of the room for the RedBrick team. It was something we always tried to do, that way the people we were presenting to didn't have to constantly move their heads back and forth, from looking at us and then looking at the screen. It also gave us a chance to see their reaction to what we were presenting.

"Alright team," I said, looking at each of them. "Without knowing it, Carrie gave us the best advice possible. We've done the prep and we know the play. Let's just be ourselves and have fun."

A few minutes later, the first team member from RedBrick arrived. As each person entered, they did a round of greetings with each of us and then took their seats. We had placed a notepad with our logo on it, a nice pen, and a copy of the presentation in front of each chair.

Once everyone was seated, Mark, their CMO, kicked things off.

"Thank you for coming in," he said. "I want to start by saying, whatever we end up deciding, we have truly appreciated your partnership over the last few years. You wouldn't be here if that wasn't the case. But you know we have a big decision to make, and we can only choose one agency partner, so if it's not your agency, I hope there are no hard feelings. We've tried to run a fair process and we're excited to see what you have to show us today."

Steve stood up and said, "Thanks, Mark, and we truly appreciate your partnership as well. We know it's a tough decision for your team, and I guess I should apologize because we're going to try to make it as difficult as possible."

The group laughed, and Steve tapped a button on his clicker. The agenda slide popped up and he talked the group through the process we'd go through in the meeting.

Then he said, "But before we begin, our CEO, Will, has some things he'd like to share."

He handed me the clicker and sat down, and I took his place in front of the room.

"I want to start by echoing what Steve said. We're honored and humbled to be meeting with you all today, and to have a chance to be your agency going forward. We have loved working with you and hope that after today, we have convinced you that we're the best partner for you to trust your brand with.

"I couldn't help but notice that you have a tremendous view of Foothills Park from this conference room," I said. The team turned to look out the window. "We have a great view of it as well from our office, although from a different viewpoint. I learned something recently about parks and the way they're designed.

"You might be surprised to learn that a successful park is one that starts with a Purpose. Why does this park need to exist? How will it be useful to the community? What does it stand for?

"Mark, you posed a similar question to me a few months back," I said, making my way back to the front of the room. "And quite frankly, at the time I didn't have a great answer. But I took your question seriously and began a journey to discover the answer."

I stepped to the side so the audience could see the projector screen, and I tapped the clicker. A video began to play with soft, inspirational music in the background. The video began by scrolling through photos of our team together in various settings—people talking and laughing together in the office, someone using a wheelbarrow at our Do Good Event, a shot of team members huddled around a pinball machine at our company office...

Over the music I said, "What I learned about our team was that, yes, we have extremely talented individuals. We have team members that have substantial experience in their craft, who come from great colleges and universities, and who are recognized in the community as being at the top of their game. But you know what? Massive can say the same thing."

The video continued to play, showing more shots of our team, as I continued. "Now, I'd put our team's capabilities against anyone's, but honestly, for a brand like yours, I think that's table stakes. You'll love the ideas we show you today just as much as I'm sure you loved the ideas that Massive presented earlier this morning.

I'm here to tell you that today, you shouldn't be choosing the agency with the best ideas. You should be choosing the agency that will be the best partner for you in the long run. The agency that will be there, side by side with you, fighting together with you to achieve your goals. What you need…is an agency with heart."

I paused as the presentation transitioned from photos to a video of the Acknowledgments portion of our most recent company meeting. The music quieted so the voices of the people giving their acknowledgments could be heard. As the video transitioned from one team member to the next sharing their love for one another, I turned to look at the RedBrick team. At one point, after a particularly moving section when a team member talked about the loss of a loved one and how supportive everyone had been, I noticed a woman toward the back wipe a tear from her eye.

The video eventually faded to black, with one voice still being heard. It was Tina saying, "I just don't know what I would do without all of you. I'm so happy coming in every day knowing that you all will be here. I just love this place."

The video ended and I let the silence fill the room for a few moments.

"I get a little choked up, too," I said, "every time I watch that. I've been trying to decipher what is special about this company for the last six months, and it wasn't until recently that it truly hit me. This is a company that has heart. We believe in each other, we trust each other, we root for each other and we pick each other up when we fall down. And we not only do that for ourselves, but we do that for our partners as well.

"I know this is a different way to start a pitch, and believe me, it made some of us," I said, smiling and tipping my head toward Steve, "a little uncomfortable when I decided to do it. But you need to know that, through the ups and downs that naturally happen in a relationship, we'll be there with you, side by side, working together to solve the problems. We'll make your goals our goals, we'll work extremely hard to build trust with your entire team, and we'll do it all because we lead with our hearts."

I looked at Mark and said, "You asked me what we stand for as a company. That's the answer. We lead with our hearts and we care about the relationships we have with each other and our partners. We truly care. And I know it might be a bit sappy, but it's the truth. Thanks for letting me share that."

As I sat down, Mark began clapping, and then his entire team joined in. The applause didn't last long, and I couldn't really tell if they meant it or if they were doing it to be polite, but I did make eye contact with Mark and he gave me an approving, "nice job" smile.

Steve then grabbed the clicker and began taking us through the rest of the presentation.

CHAPTER 35

"Everyone is buzzing about your speech at the beginning of the pitch yesterday," Rachel said as I entered the lobby. I decided to spend a few hours at The Steaming Cup before coming in, both to catch up on email and prep a little more for today's board meeting.

"Were you," I said, looking around the lobby, "waiting for me to arrive?"

"What? No, of course not," she said unconvincingly.

I began walking to my desk and she followed.

"So, about that speech…" she said.

"I wouldn't call it a speech, exactly. How did they even hear about it?"

"Oh, you know how this place works, things just…circulate. But I think you made an impression on the team that was with you because more than one of them told me about it. And Steve called it a 'drop the mic' moment," she said.

"Well, it sounds like things are being blown a bit out of proportion. But, I did take a risk, and hopefully," I said, looking at my watch, "we should find out soon if it had any impact on the result."

"You expect to hear from RedBrick today?" she asked.

"I do. Mark told me they were going to meet immediately after our presentation and make a decision. I kind of expected to hear from him last night, actually. The longer it goes before we hear, the worse our chances are," I said.

In our business, when an agency is notified that they won the account, they immediately begin contract negotiations with the client. That can take anywhere from a few days to a few weeks. During that time, some clients are hesitant to tell the agency that lost about the decision, because if they can't agree on terms with the winning agency, the agency that lost would be their backup.

So, we always become skeptical the longer it takes for a client to let us know the verdict.

"Okay, obviously I'll want to hear as soon as you find out. How are you feeling about the board meeting this afternoon?" she asked.

"Honestly, I have no idea. I know what I want to say, I just am not sure if it will work. Or for that matter, if they've already made a decision," I said.

"You think there's a chance they've made up their mind already to sell the business?" She asked.

"Normally I would have said that was an impossibility, but then again, I would have said the same thing about them ever starting this process without me being involved. At this point, I have no idea what they're thinking."

She nodded and began to walk away. Then she turned around and came back. "Oh, one more thing. Remember how I told you the data that Paul and I were collecting wasn't showing the results we expected to see? I pulled the employee sentiment data and the exit interview results to find out when our culture was suffering the most, and Paul worked with Steve to get the client data. Then we could hopefully show that when our culture was suffering the most, our client relationships and profitability were also suffering," she said.

"Yep, I remember," I said.

"Well, the weirdest thing happened. I went to Steve a few days ago to get the latest numbers, just to see if anything had occurred since he gave Paul the data a few months back," she said.

"Did you find anything?" I asked, hoping that maybe the uptick in our culture over the past few weeks might be showing an impact on our client relationships. It felt too soon but would be great data to show in the board meeting.

"No, I think there hasn't been enough time to see a change," she said. "But, I decided to go back over the data from years past just to run the numbers again, and this time the numbers *did* match up! At every point when we had a higher percentage of turnover, which the surveys showed was the result of our culture suffering, there was a direct correlation with clients being unhappy! I know, I shouldn't be excited about this, but at least our theory that culture affects client relationships is accurate."

"So, what happened with the data?" I asked. "Why was it different this time?"

"That's the weird thing. I asked Steve if that was the same data he had sent to Paul when we originally were looking at this, and he said it was. I'm guessing somehow Paul sent me the wrong information or maybe he was looking at it and sorting it in a certain way, and accidentally changed some rows or something," she said.

"True, that does happen sometimes," I said, though it wasn't like Paul to make that kind of mistake. If anything, he was overly concerned with details…

"Anyway, good luck at the board meeting!" she said, and headed down the hallway.

Thinking about what Rachel had shared, suddenly everything that had been happening over the last six months made sense. The acquisition process, the wild goose chase I had been on, the questioning of everyone and everything around me…it all pointed to one thing.

At that moment, my phone vibrated on my desk.

It was a text from Mark at RedBrick.

CHAPTER 36

Thirty minutes later, board members began showing up at the office.

Paul walked in, greeted a few of them, and then came over to me.

"Hey," he said quietly, "I thought you said you were going to share the plan with me this morning."

"Oh, sorry, I guess time got away from me. Don't worry, I've got it all figured out." Before he could respond, I said, "Looks like James just got here. We should probably get everyone into the board room."

I left him and made my way over to James. We shook hands and he said, "Hey, Will. We're really excited to see what you've come up with today."

"Does that mean you all haven't made a decision yet?" I asked, unable to resist.

He looked shocked. "Will, we told you we'd give you until this meeting to make your case. Of course we haven't made a decision."

Whew. At least there was still a chance.

Five minutes later everyone was seated around the conference room table. I had essentially been preparing for this moment for six months. Well, I thought as I swallowed hard, I was as ready as I'd ever be.

"Thank you all for being here this morning," I said. "Given the circumstances, I've decided to run this meeting a little differently. Instead of going over all the numbers, which were sent out to you a few days before the meeting as we normally do, I want to talk to you about the immense progress we've made..and then I want to show you."

Paul said, "Will, is this really necessary? I'm sure the board would rather just see our numbers and use that to decide..."

"Thanks, Paul, but we would like to follow Will's lead on this," James said. "Will, please continue."

"Great, I appreciate that," I said. I clicked the remote and a slide popped up on the screen. It read:

CREATING AN UNDENIABLE CULTURE

"When you first told me there was a chance that we'd sell the business, I'm not going to lie, it was like a slap in the face. But once I got over the initial shock, I realized that you all wouldn't have considered anything like that if you felt confident that our business was headed in the right direction. I started doing some deep reflection on the business, specifically how I was leading the business, and I realized that you were right. We were broken and needed to get back on track.

"Only, during the last six months, I realized that we never really were on track. We had no foundational elements to ensure we were building an Undeniable Culture, and instead our problems were masked by fast growth. Once that growth slowed, our problems began to become apparent," I said.

Looking around the room, I saw that everyone was still with me… everyone, that is, other than Paul. He was fiddling with his pen and was clearly uncomfortable.

"We began studying other cultures, learning both what to do and what not to do. Actually, mostly what not to do—you really have no idea how much our top competitors are getting wrong when it comes to their culture.

"Ultimately, we landed on three core focus areas, or nine steps in total, to create an Undeniable Culture. And we've been working hard to put these elements into place at our company."

I tapped the clicker again and a new screen popped up.

Undeniable Culture

Step 1: Authentic Foundation

1. Purpose, Vision, Tenets, and Values (PVTV)

2. Core Identity

3. Doing Good Together

Step 2: Trusting Team

1. Focused Leader

2. United Leadership Team

3. Active Meetings

Step 3: Inclusive Environment

1. Live the Values

2. Open Communication

3. Genuine Relationships

I then began walking them through each of the items on the screen, telling them how we've worked to bring them to life in the business. And I could tell by their questions that they were immersed and engaged.

Eventually, James said, "Will, this is great work. You and Paul have obviously been working hard to reshape the business. And honestly, the steps you listed to creating an Undeniable Culture are so impressive that I think, with your permission, I might share them with another company I'm advising."

"Absolutely, feel free to share them," I said.

"But," James said, "I think you said you were going to *show* us how these have been working in your business?"

I smiled and said, "That's right. Tell you what, let's take a five-minute break. Get some more coffee or, someone, please eat one of the pastries," I pleaded as no one ever ate the refreshments we put out, "and I'll go make sure everything is ready."

I quickly exited the conference room and checked in with Tina and Rachel. They were waiting for me in the lobby. A few minutes before the board meeting started I told them what I had planned.

“Everything is ready,” Tina said, smiling and giving me a thumbs up.

“Okay,” I said, taking a deep breath. “Here we go.”

I opened the double doors to the conference room, propped them open and said, “Okay, gang, we’re going on a little bit of a field trip. Follow me.”

A little surprised, they stood up and one by one came walking out. Once they were gathered in the lobby, I said, “What we’re going to do is walk through the office so you can feel and experience the culture. And, we’ll stop and ask a few people along the way some questions about working here.”

I looked over at Tina and gave her a nod, and she came over. “You all know Tina—she makes this place run. Now, Tina, just so the board knows whether or not this is all a set up, do you have any idea what I’m going to ask you?”

She shook her head and said, “Nope, not a clue, and honestly I’m a little nervous about it!”

Several board members laughed, and I said, “I know, putting someone on the spot in front of the board feels like a big thing, but trust me, they’re harmless. Well, most of them are harmless.” A few more laughs.

“What I’d like you to share with the board is how you feel about working at this company,” I said.

"Oh, gosh," Tina said, "well that's an easy one. You all might think because I work at the front desk I have one of the least interesting jobs in the company. But the fact is, I get to see and interact with everyone who comes in, all day long! I love my job, though recently Will asked me what I ultimately wanted to do with my career, so we're talking about that."

She looked at me and said, "And actually, Will, you should know that was a really big deal to me. You taking the time to find out what I wanted to do in the long run just made my week! I called my mom on the way home that night and told her how much that meant to me."

Turning back toward the board, she said, "And I think that's how I would answer the question of how I feel about working here. This is a place where people really care about each other. Like, truly care about one another. I can't tell you how many times I've seen someone help another team member out, or how people support each other because they really care about each other's feelings. It's a place where we all feel supported and encouraged to be ourselves. It feels…like a family, actually."

James said, "Tina, thank you for sharing that with us. It means a lot."

"Yes, thanks, Tina," I said. "Now, let's continue our tour through the office."

I led them down the long corridor and into the client services and business development area. There were 15 people in the cluster of desks, with Steve and Ahmet among them. Their old personal offices were of course empty, labeled as Conference Room 1 and Conference Room 2.

I turned toward the board and said, “These are the teams that help us win, and keep, clients. I wanted to stop here for a moment to show you how Steve, who runs client relationships, and Ahmet, who runs business development, are sitting out with the entire team.”

Steve was standing by two people’s desks talking animatedly about something. Ahmet was at his desk with his headphones on, hammering away at his laptop.

I caught Steve’s eye and waved him over.

“Hey, everyone!” Steve said, and began shaking all of their hands, like a true client partner. Looking at me he said, “What’s going on, Will? A group tour?”

“Something like that,” I said. “Can you tell the board what it’s like to not have a personal office any more?”

“Oh, sure,” he said, chuckling. He pointed at me and said to the board, “This guy and his ideas, am I right? But this one, having no one stay in personal offices, well that was a genius idea. And let me tell you, I don’t think any of us were excited about it when he first mentioned it. But then he was the first one to move out, so we were all like, how can we not if the CEO did it?!”

Bruce said, “But how do you get any work done? Don’t you need peace and quiet sometimes?”

"I wondered the same thing, Bruce. But to be honest, that hasn't been a problem. First of all, you see Ahmet over there? He doesn't even know you all are on a tour, which when he finds out he missed out on meeting you all, he's going to freak!" Steve said. "We have a policy where if someone has headphones on, they aren't to be distrubed. Some people listen to music whereas I prefer simply white noise. And we also have those two conference rooms which anyone on our team can book to get some peace and quiet.

"The thing that is so great about not being in a personal office is that I get to be out here with the entire team, all day. They're much more comfortable approaching me and I can quickly help them problem-solve because I'm so accessible. And also hearing what Ahmet's team is working on helps our teams work together better. In fact, just removing the high-walled cubicles and moving everyone into desks has increased the communication between our teams ten-fold!"

Knowing Steve could talk all day about this (or anything), I jumped in, "Steve, that's great, thanks for sharing. You'll have your team in The Farm in a few minutes?"

"Yep, sure will. Though we still don't know what for…"

"Thanks," I said. Turning to the board I said, "Okay, one more stop."

I led them further into the office and we ended up in The Farm. I paused for a moment so they could feel the buzz of activity. People were engaged in deep conversations all over, with a smattering of people in the middle of it all, headphones on, knocking out work. It was a beautiful mess of chaos and order, and it screamed creative agency.

I then opened the door to my old office, now called, "The Farm Conference Room," and said, "Let's all jump in here for a minute."

After I had moved out of my personal office, we restructured the room to have a table in the corner with six chairs around it, and we left the couch, two large chairs, and a coffee table that had always been in there.

Once all the board members entered, I closed the door and said, "I'm curious what your thoughts are so far."

Linda said, "I have to say, I really love the way it feels out there. I remember when I last went on a tour—I think that was earlier this year, maybe eight or nine months ago—when I brought my friend who had a sales opportunity to talk to you about. The energy at that time was pretty low, in fact, I remember making an excuse to my friend about it."

I nodded and said, "I remember that! She must not have been too impressed because, as you know, we didn't end up getting her account."

"Well, it's like we walked through a different company just now. There definitely seems to be a renewed sense of passion!" she said.

"What impressed me most," Bruce said, "was the conversation with Tina. She really loves working here! And I know people who work the front desk are meant to be agreeable, but you could tell she really meant it. And not many people feel the way she does about their place of work."

"I was surprised by how much Steve enjoyed being out in the open and not having his own office," Samantha added.

"And how people were able to work with their headphones on in the middle of all that chaos!" Bruce said.

There was a light knock on the door, and Tina poked her head in. "Boss, we're ready when you are," she said.

I turned toward the board and said, "Okay, there's one more thing I want you to see before we go back to the board room. We call it 'Acknowledgments.'"

Twenty minutes later we were all seated back in the conference room. Before I could say anything, Bruce spoke up.

"That," he said, "was incredible. If I hadn't seen it with my own eyes, I wouldn't have thought it was possible. Those people truly care about each other!"

The board had just experienced one of our Acknowledgments sessions and the effect had been exactly what I had hoped. The team, of course, was exuberant in their praise and recognition for one another, and several times a team member had to wipe away tears. I even caught a few board members doing the same.

The projector was still showing our plan, and Samantha looked up at it and said, “It’s clear that you have not only created a system to build an Undeniable Culture, but you’ve also been able to make incredible progress over a short period of time.”

“Yes! And imagine what we could do if we had even more time! This is why I want you to turn down the acquiring entity and stick with me for the long term. I wouldn’t have really believed this six months ago, but I’m telling you now, we have a chance to build something really special. I’m ready to pour my heart into creating a business that not only has heart and cares about its team members, but also shows consistent growth and high margins. If given the chance…”

“Will,” James said, interrupting me, “you can stop. We’re in. We met up before this meeting and said that if you could show us that you’re still passionate about building this business and if you’d made progress on improving it, then we’d back you and turn down the offer. You’ve more than proved yourself on both points. We’re ready to stick with you for the long run.”

“WHAT?!” Paul said, slamming his hands down on the table. Everyone jumped, and he said, “You have to be kidding me! The offer was incredible, and you’re falling for this… this magic act?”

He stood up and stormed out of the conference room, slamming the door behind him.

“Wow, I’m really sorry about that, everyone,” I said.

Linda said, “How did he know the offer was incredible?”

“Because, Linda,” I said, “Paul made the offer.”

CHAPTER 37

"What do you mean, Paul made the offer?" James asked.

"I only recently put it all together," I said. "Paul was in favor of selling the business the moment you all brought it up, and that should have been a bit of a red flag. But I knew he was having some financial issues and it kind of made sense, so I overlooked it.

"As you might imagine, he fought the moves I was making every step of the way, which again, wasn't really out of character but usually we find common ground when solving problems, but this time we never did. I suppose at some point he realized what I was doing was working, so he started trying to sabotage my efforts."

"What? How?" Linda asked.

"One thing he did was try to suggest that Charles was behind it all. Bruce, he saw you two having a meeting at a cafe around the corner and used that to make me think Charles was leaking information to you," I said.

"Seriously? We were just meeting about the park!" he said.

"I know. I eventually confronted Charles and he explained it all to me. But even that, I wrote off as Paul simply misunderstanding what he saw. It really all came together for me earlier today when Rachel shared incorrect data that she had received from Paul. I can understand Paul being resistant to change, but making a mistake with the data—on a critical issue of that magnitude—well that's simply unheard of."

"And then I remembered the text you showed me from the buyer," I said to Bruce. "Would you mind pulling up the latest message that he sent you?"

While Bruce pulled out his phone, I pulled out mine and opened my text messaging app.

"See, I thought there was something strange about the message when you showed it to me, but I couldn't put my finger on what it was. And then when Paul texted me earlier this morning it finally hit me."

I held my phone out to Bruce and showed him the text:

hey, i know today will probably be tough but the sale will be good for us man, trust me

"Notice anything peculiar about that?" I asked.

"I do, and now I see what you're saying," Bruce said. "It's clearly Paul that's been texting me as well."

Samantha said, "How do you know that?"

"Because he's not using any capital letters," Bruce said. "Here, look." He passed his phone around so everyone could see it.

"I've never known anyone else to write like that. I should have seen it sooner, but honestly, I'm not sure that would have helped. I needed to go on that wild goose chase to see who was behind this and meet with Codeword 9, Brainstick, and Massive. Without those meetings, I'm not sure I would have been able to get to this solution." I said, gesturing at the screen.

"Speaking of Massive, do you know anything about the RedBrick pitch?"

"Oh, yeah, that, "I said. "We won, and our revenue over the next six months will be 50% higher."

"Why didn't you tell us? That's amazing news!" Linda said.

"I thought about telling you right when we started the meeting, but honestly, I wanted you to call off the acquisition because you believed in what we were doing, not because a big win swayed you. If we're going to work together on this business, I'm going to need your support and belief in what we're trying to do," I said.

"Well, you certainly did that, and we're sorry we put you through this. You have our commitment that we'll never consider anything like this again without you being in the loop and fully on board. That was a mistake on my part, as Board Chair, and I'll own it," Bruce said, as much to the entire board as to me.

"I appreciate that, and no hard feelings, honestly. In the end, it was a needed jolt for me to see that the business *did* need to be fixed, and I needed to improve as a leader. We ended up in a much better place," I said. "Now, I probably need to go and talk with Paul. I assume we can adjourn this meeting?"

"Meeting adjourned," Bruce said.

CHAPTER 38

As I walked down the hall to Paul's office, I wasn't sure if I'd ever had such a duality of emotions. On one hand, I was beyond elated that the work the team and I had done over the last six months saved the company. And we won RedBrick's account, something I still couldn't quite believe happened. On the other hand, my partner and co-founder of the business had deceived me and tried to sell the company out from under me. And for that, I was heartbroken.

I got to his office—he still had a personal office—and knocked on the door.

"Come in," I heard Paul say. I opened the door and saw him packing his stuff up into a box. I entered and closed the door behind me.

He looked up and said, "Did you know it was me?"

"Well, I didn't really know until you freaked out in the meeting," I said. "I was pretty sure you were involved, but that certainly sealed the deal. Paul, after all we've been through, why did you do this?"

He stopped packing and slumped down into the chair behind his desk. I took a seat across from him.

"About nine months ago I was approached by a private equity firm about us possibly selling to them. I told them there was no way you'd agree to it, thinking that would be the end of it, but they came back to me with a plan to do it without you. I kept trying to reason with you that we should sell but you just wouldn't listen. Then, I guess, I just convinced myself that it was the best thing for you, for both of us, and I used that to move the process forward."

"You didn't think to just be honest with me?" I asked.

"You never would have listened to them, no matter how great the deal was—and I'm telling you, it's a great deal! You're too stubborn and I didn't think the company was salvageable. Our numbers were going in the wrong direction on all fronts—client wins were down, employee turnover was up, revenue and profit were down—and I didn't think we could turn it around.

"But mostly," he said, looking up at me with pain in his eyes, "I realized I just didn't believe in *you* any more."

Those words hurt me like nothing had ever hurt me before. I couldn't speak.

After a few moments, Paul said, "Look, I know I can't stay here after what I did, and you deserve a partner who you can build trust with, and…"

"And who believes in me?" I asked.

"Yes," Paul said, "who believes in you. I'm sorry it's come to this, I really am."

"Me, too," I said, standing up. "In a few days I'll reach out to you with an offer to buy out your stock."

I walked to the door and opened it. Before I could leave, Paul said, "Hey, Will, I know it doesn't mean much at this point, but after today's board meeting, I actually think you can do this. It's a great plan you've put in place and I'm going to be rooting for you."

I gave him a half-smile, which was all I could muster, and I stepped out of his office and closed the door.

SIX MONTHS LATER

Uh, Charles, is this really a good idea?" I asked as I snapped the helmet on my head.

We were standing at the bottom of the skateboarding bowl in Foothills Park, along with a few other adults. The instructor who was running the class, called "You're not too old to skateboard," was motioning everyone over to her on the other end of the bowl.

"Oh, what are you worried about? We have helmets, knee pads, elbow pads…heck, this is safer than walking at this point!" he said.

I was pretty sure that when Charles asked me to do this with him, I only said yes because I still felt guilty about doubting him earlier in the year. After this, I was going to call us even.

I followed him over to the instructor. Once everyone had gathered around, she said, "Now, I know what you're thinking, and don't worry, none of you will be breaking any bones on my watch. That only happens about 50% of the time, and since someone broke their arm yesterday in my class, you all should be safe."

She looked around at the group, with our wide eyes bulging out of our heads, and said, "I'm kidding! Jeez, you guys really are scared about this! No one has ever broken a bone in my class, and I don't intend to start today."

Hilarious.

The next hour went by quickly and I only fell a few times, resulting in, as the instructor predicted, no broken bones. We practiced simple things like pushing off, kick turns and carving turns, and before we were done Charles even managed to do an ollie, which blew me away.

After the class we found a park bench to sit on, drinking the water that the instructor passed out after the class.

"I have to admit, that was fun," I said.

Charles said, "You know, they have a weekly class that you can join…"

"Not," I interrupted, "that fun. I think I'll stick with having my feet firmly planted on the ground."

He laughed and said, "Yeah, it's not really for me either. But it was good to get on a skateboard again. I think it's been, what, maybe 30 years since I stood on a skateboard! Wow, time really does fly. Speaking of which, it's been about six months since…well, since everything happened with you! Since you won over the board, since Paul left the company, since you won RedBrick…"

He was right. I couldn't believe it had already been half a year since all of that happened. So much had changed in my life over the last six months.

"And I know we've talked about it since, but I'm curious now that you have some space, how you're feeling about everything," he said.

"It's amazing to think about what my business was like a year ago and what it is like today. A few things have happened since we last met up, by the way. I promoted Rachel to COO, finally.

She's been such a great partner and it was high time she had that role," I said.

"I'm not surprised. She's got so much potential. Your job now is to make sure you keep giving her opportunities to keep growing," he said.

"Agreed. And I finally negotiated a deal with Paul to buy out his shares. I got a loan from the bank—thanks for the introduction to the bank president, that helped a lot—and sent him the payment last week," I said.

"No problem. Sam's a great guy, glad that worked out," he said. "So, how are you and Paul? Any progress on the relationship?"

I shook my head and said, "No. I mean, I'm sure we'll get back to some kind of relationship, but between my disappointment and anger toward him for what he did, and his shame in having done it, I'm not sure how we'll ever get back to being friends again."

I looked over at him and said, "By the way, I was talking with Sarah the other day about all of this, reflecting on what happened, and it reminded me of something I wanted to ask you. When all of that stuff started happening with the board and the acquisition, you seemed to be hinting at the fact that it might be Paul, but I wasn't picking up the hint. At least, I think you were."

He smiled and said, "Now why would you think that?"

"Well, you said something about keeping my eyes open and being aware of what was happening around me. And at one point you seemed to understand how the acquiring company might be able to buy the business without me being attached…"

"Yes, when you said that, the only way I could see that being possible was if Paul was going to stay on as CEO or would help find the next CEO, which meant he had to somehow be involved," he said.

"Then why didn't you tell me?" I asked.

"Because," he said, looking at me, "you needed to figure it out on your own, *if* that was even what was happening. I couldn't be sure, and even suggesting that your business partner could be trying to take the company away from you could cause a rift between you two that could have ruined everything. The last thing I'd ever want to do, based only on an assumption, is break up your partnership. So I decided to keep my mouth shut and let you figure it out. Which you did just in the nick of time, I might add."

I thought about that for a minute and said, "That makes sense, and I appreciate you letting me work it out. Beyond that, our focus on building an Undeniable Culture is working out terrifically. RedBrick has continued to be happy, and the account is growing even beyond what we expected! And I go into work every day excited and energized, which is a great feeling to have again."

"That's wonderful, Will," Charles said, standing up. "It's time for me to head out. Let's plan to get together again in about a month. I heard about this great little rock climbing place that just opened…"

Shaking my head and laughing, I said, "No way! I thought I just got done telling you that I wanted to keep my feet on the ground!"

We shook hands and he hopped on his bike and pedaled away. I stepped onto the path and began walking back toward the office.

As I neared the exit, I noticed someone had placed a sticker on one of the huge stone columns marking the entrance to the park.

Somehow, I thought to myself, it felt like I was just beginning my journey as a leader…

YOU MADE IT TO THE END!

Thank you for reading this book. Honestly, there are a million other books out there to read and the fact that you took the time to read this book means the world to us.

(If you have a few more minutes to spare, we'd be so appreciative if you'd consider putting a review on Amazon and GoodReads. Reviews help others find the book, plus they make us feel good.)

It's quite possible this is the last book I will write about Will, Rachel, and the rest of the gang. But if there is one thing I've learned on this journey, it's that I have no idea what direction this will head.

As I mentioned in the Prelude, I'm excited to dive into Charles's background and explore his journey through a book I'm currently calling, *The Life Turnaround.* And there's something about Rachel that intrigues me, so perhaps I'll think about that more in the future....

If you have ideas or suggestions, please email my publishing company, Ripples Media, at contact@ripples.media. We'd love to know what you'd like in future books and/or any general suggestions you might have about how we could be doing a better job.

ACKNOWLEDGMENTS

Jeff

I first want to acknowledge the Ripples Media team for being such amazing partners on this journey: Rachelle Kuramoto, Dorothy Miller-Farleo (DMF), and our newest rockstar, Andrew Vogel. You are all incredible and I'm honored to be in the arena with you.

To Adam Albrecht, my co-author of this book, who helped me build a pretty great culture at Engauge once upon a time. If there's a person that exudes "great culture!" it's Adam.

To Ryan Gravel, for helping me understand the nuances of creating a purposeful park and civic area in a community (and for being such a great leader in Atlanta!).

To Jeff Maggs, for letting me use his name (how great is the name, "Maggs"?) in the book. What a funny conversation that was: "Hey Maggs, are you cool if I use your last name for a character in my next book? He's an agency leader, like you, but unlike you, he's unfocused and indecisive. I'll make sure to tell everyone what a great leader you are in the Acknowledgements." The real Jeff Maggs is not just a nice guy, but has a great vision for leading his team :)

To Raj Choudhury, Danny Davis, and Donovan and Jenni Panone, for those super early years at Spunlogic when we were basically babies trying to run a company, and all we ever wanted was for people to love working at the company. We hardly used the word "culture," but we knew in our core it was all that really mattered. Those were some of the best days of my life.

And lastly, but most importantly, to my family (the 7mires): Emily, Zac, Drew, Kaitlyn, Hannah, and Kai. If there was something called a "home culture" (maybe there should be.... hm, another book perhaps?) we'd be knocking it out of the park. I love you all.

Adam

Thank you to my University of Wisconsin track and field coaches Mark Napier and Ed Nuttycombe, for showing me how culture leads to championships. And to my Badger teammates for embracing that winning culture.

Thanks to my parents Robert and Jill Albrecht, for creating our family culture.

To Jeff Hilimire, who is a constant reminder to put people first and everything else will take care of itself.

To my wife Dawn and kids, Ava, Johann, and Magnus, for contributing to our fun, funny and wonderful culture at home.

ABOUT THE AUTHORS

Jeff Hilimire is the best-selling author of *The Turnaround Leadership Series* and an accomplished entrepreneur who has launched multiple organizations and successfully sold two companies. He is currently the Board Chair of Dragon Army, an award-winning digital engagement agency, and is the CEO of Purpose Group, a purpose-driven private equity firm focused on bringing PVTV™ to small businesses across the United States.

He is also the co-founder and board member of two nonprofit organizations. 48in48 is a global nonprofit that produces hackathon events, building 48 nonprofit websites in 48 hours. The A Pledge creates a path for systemic opportunity in Atlanta by inspiring marketing and advertising agencies to commit to matching the diversity of their team to that of our city by 2030.

Jeff lives in Atlanta with his wife, Emily, and their five children. You can follow Jeff's adventures on his personal blog, jeffhilimire.com, or sign up for his newsletter at jeffhilimire.com/newsletter.

Adam Albrecht is the author of *What Does Your Fortune Cookie Say?* as well as the founder and CEO of the advertising and ideas agency The Weaponry. The agency's portfolio of clients ranges from legendary international brands to innovative startups. Prior to The Weaponry, he worked at renowned advertising agencies Cramer-Krasselt, Engauge Marketing and Moxie, in roles ranging from copywriter to Chief Creative Officer.

Adam has worked on iconic brands including Reddi-Wip, Nike, Coca-Cola, Dasani, Nationwide Insurance, Wells Fargo, UPS, Hertz, Safelite, Mizuno, Bob Evans, Chick-fil-A, GNC, Universal Studios, AMC Theatres, Volvo, Prevost, SeaDoo, Ski-Doo, and Can-Am.

Adam earned a double major in journalism and psychology from the University of Wisconsin. He also captained the Badgers' Big Ten Conference champion track and field team, becoming the No. 1 hammer thrower and No. 4 discus thrower in school history.

Adam lives in Milwaukee with his wife Dawn and children Ava, Johann, and Magnus. You can follow Adam at adamalbrecht.blog, where he shares ideas on self-improvement, creativity, and entrepreneurship.

ABOUT THE SERIES

BE THE LEADER YOU ALWAYS WANTED TO BE.

Get to know Will and his team as they navigate the opportunities and challenges of a competitive and crowded marketplace. This book, while the fourth in *The Turnaround Leadership Series*, happens first in chronological order.

Blending a narrative style with helpful insights and actionable tools, as well as drawing from the author's 25 years of leading companies, *The Turnaround Leadership Series* is a great resource for leaders looking to foster organizational growth, cohesive cultures, and sustainable results, in order to create real Purpose in their business.

"By using PVTV, we created a guiding purpose, a vision, and tenets we could be proud of to share with our partners."

Megan Barney, Sr. Director of Planning & Execution for Global Product Management, Digital Platforms at Equifax

"Jeff makes the connection between the need for teams to shoot for a higher purpose and to embrace values with the need for an operational system."

Jack Stack, CEO of SRC Holdings Corporation and best-selling author of The Great Game of Business *and* A Stake in the Outcome

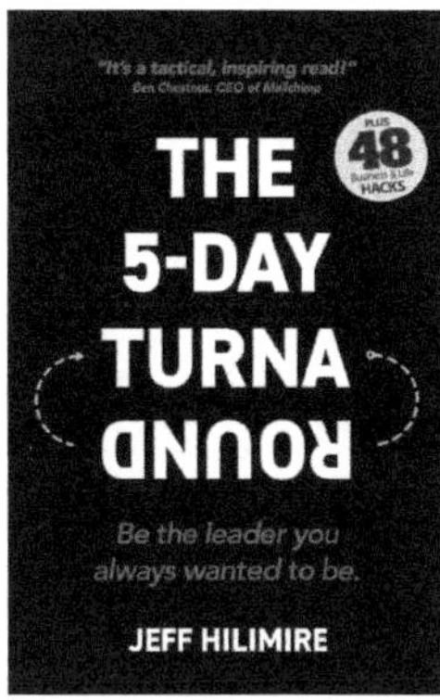

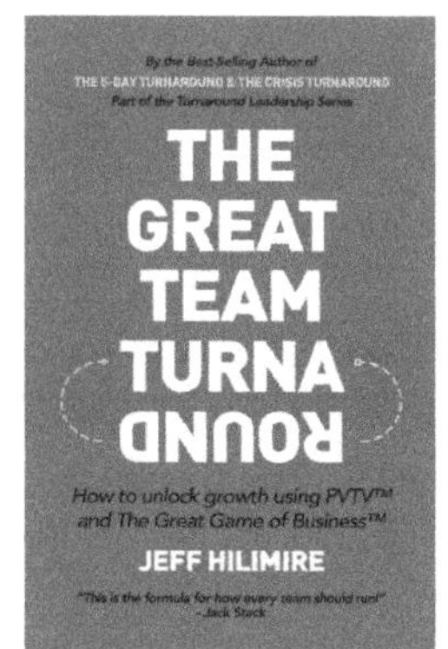

Create Transformative Growth

For large companies, following well-established processes is deemed necessary for securing the bottom line. But what happens when pursuing the status quo slows progress or, worse yet, creates a setback? ***The 5-Day Turnaround*** offers actionable steps for driving growth by thinking and acting like an entrepreneur, even inside mid-sized and enterprise organizations.

Lead Confidently Through Crisis

Most leaders plan for emergencies. But when a crisis hits, it brings unexpected challenges. In ***The Crisis Turnaround,*** Will and his team navigate disruptions to processes, projects, revenues, and teams that come as the result of an unprecedented event. The book is a case study that prepares readers to thrive in crisis and even emerge stronger.

Putting Purpose Into Practice

The leadership classic The Great Game of Business (GGOB) has inspired countless organizations to operate with transparency and rigor. The first two books in the Turnaround Leadership Series introduce the Purpose, Vision, Tenets & Values (PVTV) model. In ***The Great Team Turnaround***, these powerful concepts come together to unlock a team's unstoppable potential.

All of *The Turnaround Leadership Series* books are available on Amazon. If you're interested in booking Jeff Hilimire for a speaking engagement, buying a bulk order for your team, or getting signed copies of any of the books, please reach out to Ripples Media at contact@ripples.media or visit www.ripples.media.

OTHER TITLES FROM RIPPLES MEDIA

Inspiring Lessons on Personal Growth

Through stories and simple action steps, ***What Does Your Fortune Cookie Say?*** educates, entertains, and inspires. Adam Albrecht, CEO of The Weaponry, offers useful ways to become a better professional and human through bite-size stories, perspective-altering ideas, thought-provoking suggestions, and reliable techniques for personal growth.

Create a Culture of Innovation

While most companies value innovation, their corporate cultures hinder actual solutions from reaching the market. Michael McCathren, who leads the Chick-fil-A innovation center, uses research, case studies, and applications to detail the best-selling ***6Ps of Essential Innovation*** that are necessary to produce and sustain a resilient innovation organization.

Living a Big Life and Leading With Love

As a brand transformation expert, award-winning marketing executive Jo Ann Herold has the unique perspective as someone who was the sole woman in the room for many years. In her new bestseller, ***Living on a Smile,*** which is part memoir and part leadership guide, she offers actionable lessons and takeaways for living and working with purpose, passion, and authenticity.